GIRL CODE

Ethics as a Lifestyle

HAZEL-E
WITH BRITTANI WILLIAMS

THE TMG FIRM

New York

The TMG Firm, LLC
112 W. 34th Street
17th and 18th Floors
New York, NY 10120
www.thetmgfirm.com

Girl Code: Ethics As A Lifestyle
Copyright © 2016 Arica Adams
Copyright © 2016 Brittani Williams
Published and edited by The TMG Firm, LLC

For more information about special discounts for bulk purchase, please contact The TMG Firm at 1-888-984-3864 ext 12 or publishing@thetmgfirm.com

ISBN: 978-0-99835-653-2
Library of Congress Control Number: 2016963017
All rights reserved

First The TMG Firm Trade Paperback Edition April 2017
Printed in the United States of America

Cover Photo Copyright © 2016 Hernan Rodriguez for Hernan Photography Studios
Cover created and designed by Brittani Williams for TSPub Creative, LLC.

Welcome to Hazel-E's Girl Code!

FOREWORD

When I think about the state of sisterhood today, I am overwhelmed with acute nostalgia for the time when women fought for family bonds, appreciated female camaraderie, had each other's backs and respected one another. Unfortunately, we reside in an era where those characteristics are no longer a priority. Women have failed to lead by example and disregard the 'we ride for each other' ideal. Instead, they are overtaken by a 'dog eats dog' mentality. The sisterhood state of affairs has been twisted into just that...a mental state of 'affairs.' Women have lost their way in an attempt to secure amongst other things: financial status, the house, the car...the man! Even if he's already someone else's man. Everything else has become expendable, including self-respect, social conduct, and friendships.

Girl Code is a unique approach to educating women who may have forgotten that life is built upon the significant bonds of loyalty. These bonds should be upheld to enlighten our young sisters on proper etiquette, which will form lasting interpersonal relationships.

—Tami Roman
    Actress, entrepreneur, author & TV personality

GIRL CODE:

Ethics as a Lifestyle

You have now cracked the Code.

Your access has been granted.

The Girl Code is an unspoken code of conduct by which all women should strive to abide.

Unity is underrated in this day and age, but through this journey, we will learn to remember what the word 'Sisterhood' truly means. We shall remain QUEENS at all times, even when the crown seems too heavy to bear. As strong women, we will own our rights and pledge our allegiance to feminism. We shall stand together and will not bow to anyone!

THE GIRL CODE
UNSPOKEN RULES OF FRIENDSHIP

1. Never date your friend's ex-boyfriend.
2. Never befriend your ex's new girlfriend with a hidden agenda.
3. Never steal each other's style. Be original and unique.
4. Never reveal any of your friends' secrets.
5. Never socialize with enemies of your friends.
6. Never post or share unflattering photos of your friends.
7. Keep your friends close and your frenemies closer.
8. Never leave an intoxicated friend by herself.
9. Birds of a feather flock together.
10. Be there to hold each other's hand in a time of need.
11. Be there to celebrate each other's big moments.
12. Always have each other's back.
13. Don't choose a relationship over a true friendship.

14. Be a wing woman when necessary.
15. Challenge each other, but never compete.
16. Be there to support each other's career.
17. Always compliment each other.
18. Never allow anyone to talk about your friends. If you allow that you are just as guilty.
19. Never allow someone to attack your friend's credibility.
20. Always be a shoulder to cry on.
21. Be there when she needs you.
22. Always be honest. The truth is always better than a lie.
23. Watch out for your friends when they are on a date with someone new.
24. Listen to your friend vent when she needs you to.
25. Be there for each other when you go through relationship problems.
26. Never allow your friends to go out in public without being presentable.
27. Only give constructive criticism.
28. Never be jealous of each other.

29. Always let your friend know how much she means to you, even when she gets on your last nerve.

Bond of Sisterhood, Forever Friendships, and Frenemies

When speaking about women and sisterhood, we think of close relationships. In today's society, many women do not form lasting relationships. Real sisterhood isn't something that happens overnight. It takes time and effort to build a long lasting friendship. By definition, sisterhood is the state of a being a sister or having a sisterly relationship. It is also the solidarity of women based on shared conditions, experiences, or concerns. When you build an unconditional sisterly love with one another, it is one of the most rewarding relationships you could ever have. When sisterhood is true and genuine, it doesn't need to be forced. Some real friendships grow closer than the relationships we have with blood relatives. These are the women who will listen when you need an ear, get you focused when you're off track, and pass you the wine and tissue when you need to cry.

'Sisterhood' is from your heart, and it isn't a title to be taken lightly. Sisterhood should make you a better version of you. This bond should be valued because these relationships come around once in a lifetime. The idea of sisterhood is synonymous with sororities. The women of sororities are bound by their values, rituals, and bonds of sisterhood. When you join a sorority, your membership lasts for a lifetime. You can rest assured your soros will always have your back when you need them. Another important factor of sisterhood is being able to remain friendly and stay away from negativity. You should also focus on being very honest and transparent. Sisterhood isn't about being nice; it's about wanting to see another woman walk in her divine purpose and supporting her along the way.

There are many benefits of friendship. Friends make our lives better because of the impact they have on our happiness. As women, we share special bonds with each other. We bare our souls to one another and continually encourage each other to be better. Sisterhood is proven to be very empowering because it allows another woman to show you loyalty and support. When a woman in empowered she can change the world. We can connect with our sisters and share our gifts and knowledge with each other. Women must learn to love themselves before they love each other as sisters. When you are comfortable enough to call a woman your sister you are showing her that you can trust her with your life. You know she would have your back, catch you before you fall, and you would do the same for her. You are telling her that you believe in her and you are there to support her goals and aspirations. Being part of a sisterhood means sharing your secrets with the women you trust. You know you would guard her secrets with your life, and she will do the same in return. Sisterhood plays a significant role in our lives. It is important to know surrounding yourself with greatness will make you more inclined to become great. If you are to be influenced by anyone it should be someone who has all of the traits you desire for yourself.

There may be times in our lives where we feel alone. We sit, look around and realize we don't have anyone to converse with about topics we want to discuss. There is nothing worse than having much to say with no one to speak with about it. Change can make us uncomfortable. Uncertainty is never something easy to deal with, especially when you have goals to accomplish. Often, many of us don't have access to good support systems. When a friend supports you and cheers you on, it helps you to want to succeed. With sisterhood, you will always have someone in which to share your experiences. It is always great to have a friend to create those memories with, whether it's a day shopping at the mall or a vacation in Cancun.

As we navigate through life, we experience many different ups and downs. There will be those individuals who love and appreciate us, and those who will envy us and want us to fail. When you have a friend you can call your sister, she will be there for you through thick and thin. She is always in your corner and wants nothing but the best for you. It's an amazing feeling to have a woman that will stand by your side even when you haven't made the best decisions in your life. Women have always been stereotyped as being emotional. I disagree with this stigma and believe we are 'masters of our emotions.' Sometimes we make decisions without thinking of the repercussions, but that's not a 'woman trait' that's a 'human trait.' When a woman realizes she's made the wrong choice that changes the course of her life, she may become depressed. It is the job of a sister to step in and let her know that she should keep moving forward. She would never let you get discouraged. For everything you can say negatively about yourself, she can tell you at least two things about you that are positive. She will make you laugh when all you want to do is cry. She will hug you when all you want to do is scream. She would never let you stand alone in a time of adversity, and she would risk her safety if that meant keeping you out of harm's way.

A sister would always say when you are wrong, and she'll never let you make a fool of yourself. Within this sisterhood, you will hold each other accountable for your actions. When you know each other inside and out, she could probably talk you out of doing something before you say you're going to do it. She knows you like the back of her hand, and she would never let you make a mistake that could hurt your morals or values. Instead of telling her what to do, you would make sure she knows you'll support whatever decision she chooses to make.

A sisterhood is more than just being friends. It isn't with someone you only see at work or someone you only see once in a while. Of course, there will be times when both of you may be moving in different directions. We get older, get married, have children and change careers. This is a part of life, so it is possible to lose touch with some of your friends. However, the ones you call sisters still answer your calls regardless of how much time may have passed. As sisters, you could pick up right where you left off. They will still be there to support you or help you if you have a problem and need their support. There are times where we need them because they provide us with a comfort. You can always relax and be yourself when you are around them because they would never judge you and appreciate the time you spend together. You can act silly and laugh at things you may never be comfortable laughing at with others. You can relax and watch a movie, or you can get manicures together and reminisce about old times. You know each other best, and they know the real you, which makes you all worry-free in each other's company.

Think about the many times in your life when you needed advice. When things get tough, the answers to your problems may not be obtainable.

It can be confusing when you are upset and difficult to make the right choice. Who could you call? You could ask your family or your parents, but you may be afraid they will judge you. No one ever wants to feel as if they are being 'kicked while they are down.' You want to be supported even if they don't agree with your decisions. It's more beneficial to get advice from the people who know you best. It may take a little trial and error to find out who those people are. The women in your immediate circle should be able to give you advice from a different frame of reference. Having a diverse group of friends will benefit you in the long run. This circle of friends will be able to tell you what is best for you even when you don't want to accept the truth.

Sisterhood is powerful because there is strength in numbers. When experiencing issues, you may not be as strong as when you're standing alone. A group of women standing together can inspire other women to do the same. It's easy to feel as if you don't belong when you are around people you don't know very well. This is why encouraging each other is necessary. You should never feel like you don't fit in because of some disadvantages. Nor should you feel as if you have to overcompensate to meet them. When you surround yourself with like-minded, intelligent women who are different, you can pull information from each other. It's a very rewarding feeling to have a wealth of knowledge at your fingertips. Another one of the most valuable rewards of a sisterhood is pushing each other. There are times when we want to give up, but having a woman who stands behinds you and affirms that you can do it, is an immense feeling.

To have what is called a 'forever friendship,' you must make yourself vulnerable and be an open book. This is a scary feeling for most people. The thought of being vulnerable makes you susceptible to being hurt by someone. We have to be willing to take the risk to gain someone that will be by our side. When you think of a forever friendship, what comes to mind is befriending someone who will reciprocate unconditional love. We are all guilty of doing more talking than listening. She'll listen to you just as much as you listen to her. When you gain a friend, who gives you her undivided attention, it's something to treasure. It is very easy to tune someone out, especially when you have a lot on your mind. This kind of friend will never have to fear what she's saying is not being taken into consideration. She will listen to what is bothering you regardless of how bad her day has been. Most importantly, she will never get tired of listening to your concerns and issues. This is a sigh of relief as you will never feel like you're going to implode from holding everything in. This type of friendship will give us security and the fulfillment of being loved. She wants you to give her everything she has given to you, and she intends to hold onto your friendship forever.

To have a forever friend, you must be trustworthy. This is something many people battle within themselves. In the ways of the world, there are many dishonest people. At some point and time, we have all told someone an untruth. Some things happen in our lives that we may never want to tell anyone. It could become stressful when you have to hold it in without an outlet to vent. Having that person to share everything with makes a huge difference in your life. There are plenty of studies that say women are terrible at keeping secrets. There are just as many men who can't hold water either. The truth is, there are far less who even in death would never divulge your secrets. This is why it is vital to be sure they won't spread your business before telling them your entire life story. Whatever you need from your forever friend including trust, will never be an issue.

To have a forever friend, you will have to refrain from passing judgment. Since you know everything about each other, it is tempting to judge one another's choices. You are entitled to having your opinion, but making them feel judged is insupportable. Whatever you do, make sure you have a clear understanding. Keep in mind; you are different and won't always agree with each other. Disagreements are expected, so your reactions need to be appropriate. The point is, you should listen and accept what she wants for herself. She should be content with knowing that no matter what she chooses to do, you will be there by her side.

A forever friendship is only possible when both of you respect each other's values. 'Birds of a feather flock together,' so this may be one of the main reasons you are friends. This isn't only regarding behavior, but your likes, dislikes and your views on life in general. You won't always like the things she says and does, but you have to respect her for who she is. If you aren't willing to accept it, it would most likely not turn into a forever friendship.

In sisterhood, you reflect on those relationships that are the complete opposites. We've all have people who associate themselves with us and claim to be our friends. These are those that force a smile instead of clapping when you have succeeded at something. These are the women that are phony and using us for personal gain. They're antagonists 'disguised' as friends. Even more, they are low-key rivals and competitors. Their sole purpose is to be around you to ruin things. Normally, they're able to fool you for quite some time. Usually, you'll have to get hurt by them in some way before you realize who they are. There are some tell-tale signs. If you pay close attention, you'll be able to get rid of them before they cause significant damage in your life. Be wary of the people who are friendly despite their dislikes and competing with you.

A frenemy is someone who spends the majority of their time tearing you down. She will criticize you in an attempt to make herself feel better. Always siding with those who are against you, and never defending you even when the other person is wrong.

A frenemy is someone who gives you fewer reasons to be confident and more reasons to be doubtful. She'll point out all of your flaws including those you didn't even recognize. If you come to her with great news, she'll act as if it isn't that big of a deal.

A frenemy is someone who talks about you behind your back. She won't waste any time sabotaging your friendships and relationships with other people. She'll also be ready and willing to listen when someone has something negative to say about you.

A frenemy is someone who takes everything you say personally. She'll never give you the benefit of the doubt and always assumes you have negative intentions. She always thinks you are speaking about her in an unsympathetic manner and overreacts to everything you say.

A frenemy is someone who always speaks to you in a condescending tone. She often treats you as if you are a child or someone that isn't on her level. She'll demean you in front of other people without considering your feelings to prove she's superior.

A frenemy is someone who always ignores your needs. She always put her needs and feelings before yours. Every situation is always about her.

A frenemy is someone who consistently makes subliminal posts about you on social media. All of her posts are filled with subliminal attacks directed toward you. She'll find a way to embarrass you publicly and claim it was an inadvertent mistake.

A frenemy is someone who is very insensitive. She'll make you feel terrible about every one of your life choices. She'll make you feel even worse when things don't work out well for you.

A frenemy is someone who is never there for you when you need them. You could call, text, email, or show up to her front door and she'll always be unavailable. The moment she is in need, she'll immediately get in contact with you. She is selfish and will never give a fraction of what you've given to her.

A frenemy is someone who never listens to what you have to say without attacking you. You'll feel as if you have to 'walk on eggshells' to have a productive discussion with her.

A frenemy always wants to know all of your business, but will not tell you much about hers. She questions you to gain ammunition to use against you at a later date.

A frenemy always 'throws shade.' She'll mask it as a concern when in actuality she could care less about you or how you feel.

A frenemy is someone who never invites you anywhere. She attends functions and events regularly but never asks you to accompany her. She'll claim she called or texted you knowing she didn't make any attempt. But she makes herself available whenever you go out to have fun.

A frenemy is someone who doesn't have an issue with flirting or being inappropriate with your ex. She'll claim it's innocent, and make it her business always to be near your ex.

A frenemy is someone who is always looking for a way to get 'one up on you.' She'll make sure she figures out what you are doing, so she can work on a strategy to get ahead of you.

A frenemy is someone who loves to have the spotlight. She is what some would call an 'attention seeker.' She always attempts to outshine you and becomes offended when you speak to her about it. If someone focuses on you; she becomes upset. She even focuses on getting the attention of any person you are interested in or may be interested in you.

It will hurt when you have been betrayed by someone you considered a friend. Finding out the person you would do almost anything for was dishonorable makes you feel alone. There is never any excuse to treat someone badly. The truth is, many people in this world don't know how to be anything other than who they are. If you find yourself in this situation, you have to be honest with yourself. Accept losing the person because she was never a friend to you anyway. People like this end up without a support system themselves. You can't intentionally deceive and hurt someone then expect a positive outcome. Maintain your self-confidence and protect your integrity. The first thing you need to do is realize that it was never a true friendship. It's common for people to have disagreements and take time away from each other. But a real friend would never set out to harm you in any way. If you can identify a good friend and differentiate between a frenemy; you'll be aware the next time someone similar attempts to enter your life. Being in this situation could help you identify your ways in a friendship. It's possible; there may have been a time you weren't the best friend you could've been.

You may become nostalgic and remember some of the good times you shared. Do your best to think about these less and less. Never allow yourself to feel guilty for something that wasn't your fault. The next thing you should do is 'let it go.' You'll most likely be very angry, hurt or even confused. You should be able to sit down and have a discussion with her about it. You may feel she doesn't deserve to speak with you. Decide what is best for you. If you choose to speak with her, have a conversation to share your feelings and then let her know you're ceasing all communication afterward. You could let her know the friendship has run its course. This has to happen without it escalating to physical violence. Otherwise, it may be best to leave it alone in its entirety. Either way, trust your gut and intuition because they will lead you in the right direction. Any lost friendship will leave a void and sometimes it will take time to get over. You may have different emotions and question the decision you've made. As tough as it may be, you must take solace in knowing you've walked away for the right reasons. Toxic relationships can make you believe almost anything. Unfortunately, this happens all the time. You are moving forward to be mentally and emotionally healthy. Drama is never something you need to keep in your life. Know that you did the right thing for you. You'll experience some sadness, hurt, and disappointment; but time heals all wounds.

After you've been able to move on, you'll have learned what to do within future friendships. You have to focus on building strong bonds and meaningful relationships. Once you shed all of the negative energy and move forward, you will increase your positive experiences. At this point, it's important to create new habits. 'Old habits die hard,' but it isn't impossible to leave them behind. You can look for some new and exciting activities to clear your mind. Sometimes, you may not need to find other friends because you can always be a friend to yourself. Get to know who you are, what makes you happy and what makes you sad. Learn to entertain yourself. Loving yourself is very instrumental in living a happy life. It is crucial when it comes to getting over the loss of a friendship. Look for positive experiences you can enjoy by yourself. Once you add more personal goals you want to achieve, focusing on them can make you feel much better about yourself. The most important thing you must remember is with hurt you need time and space. Maybe at some point in the future, you could be open to a friendship with someone else. Only time can properly determine the possibility.

Now that you are passed the toxic friendship, you don't need to waste time talking about the past. You don't have to tell everyone about it and convince them to choose a side. There may be times when you run into the person in public. The most logical approach is to be civil and mature. Even if she decides she wants to act foolishly and unruly; you can't stoop to her level. The end of the friendship does not mean you have to go to war. You don't need to get into a verbal or physical altercation. Be the bigger person and do your best to be polite. If you can avoid the drama, you will show her she no longer has any power over you. Your goal is to be a much happier person that will cease to be influenced by her toxic ways.

Let's be clear, friends have disagreements, and sometimes we provoke and annoy each other. There aren't any friendships or relationships that haven't been through some turmoil. What makes us stronger, is the ability to go through a storm and come out on the other side closer than before. There are certain things to avoid when you have a quarrel with your best friend, to prevent permanent damage to your friendship. Sometimes we say things in the heat of the moment we don't mean. To avoid this, you should think before you speak. If for some reason you slip up and say something you don't mean, you should apologize without hesitation. If you walk away and both of you are still angry, avoid being vindictive. You should never want to get revenge for something said in the heat of an argument. Take the time to cool down and then try to patch things up.

Most importantly, avoid making your disagreement known to everyone. There's no need to rant on social media about what occurred between the two of you in private. You may feel some relief after venting, but that could make things worse. You shouldn't think you can 'sweep things under the rug' and act as if they never happened. If there were a problem, it would have to be addressed at some point. It would be better to wait until both of you have calmed down to avoid a confrontation. Try to avoid yelling because that could be the catalyst in sparking a debacle. It's a must to 'check your ego at the door' and understand that being stubborn won't remedy anything.

It is important to apologize when you are in the wrong. Make sure your apology is sincere and genuine. Even though you've apologized, you need to be sure that it won't happen again. Once you have sorted out your problems as mature adults, the healing process will begin. Reflect on where you may have gone wrong and figure out how to avoid a recurrence. Take the time to comprehend why you two were angry and use it as a learning experience. Having an in-depth discussion about it is necessary to prevent future disagreements. Once all of this has been worked out, plan some girl time where you two can have some fun and get back to enjoying each other's company. The sooner you utilize these tools, the better.

There are many unspoken rules of friendship. There are some that can keep your bond strong and some that can break it apart. We've all had friendships that at some point without warning went left. We have also built some very healthy friendships we never expected to flourish. We never know what the future may bring. We will also never be able to prepare for the twists and turns that our friendships may take. The point is if your goal is to build a bond of sisterhood it is important to be the best friend you can be. If you want to build forever friendships, you will have to work at them. It is seldom for a forever friendship to automatically fall into place. Invest your time into those who will invest their time into you. You need to foster the productive friendships and detach yourself from the ones bringing negativity into your life.

Ladylike Behavior

Ladylike, by definition, is a characteristic of a well-mannered woman or girl who adheres to traditional norms of propriety and femininity. When speaking of traditional standards, ladylike behavior has always been one of the greatest qualities a woman could possess. Being a female doesn't mean that a girl will grow up to be a 'lady.' In a world where women are encouraged to degrade and devalue themselves, the only thing you can guarantee is if you live long enough, you might just become a woman. There is a quote that reads: "Being female is a matter of birth, being a woman is a matter of age, but being a lady is a matter of choice."

The truth of the matter is that the influence of

television and social media makes more young women forgo ladylike behaviors. By a long shot, it isn't an easy process. With so much temptation on a daily basis, it will take a strong woman to develop into a lady. As parents, you'd encourage your daughters to maintain certain characteristics. Sure it is easy to become a carbon copy of what you see on TV, but it is harder to remain unique. For most, there isn't much time invested in this process. We assume that because of our sex, our instincts will guide us in the right direction. This assumption is incorrect since you can never be sure of the direction a female will choose. Each woman is different, therefore, what works for some will not work for others. It is important to know that is takes maturing to adapt ladylike behavior. It also means that this should be a requirement for young women. We shouldn't allow them to drift too far away because most likely it will be hard to get them back.

There are some things that a lady will understand that an immature young woman won't. A lady will know why her appearance, behavior as well as her communication skills are a reflection of her true character. A lady is valuable in many ways, and she can provide other women with valuable insight. A lady is confident; she knows that her real beauty lies beneath all of the makeup and clothing. She knows that her inner qualities are more precious than gold. A lady if very aware of her strength. Her strength isn't solidified by depending on a man. Her priorities in life are adapting the traits of a lady as well as being gracious, confident, intelligent and poised. To understand these traits or behaviors, we will need to break them into subsections. All of these ladylike behaviors fall under the following categories: her personality, her behavior as it relates to relationships, her appearance, and health, and how she presents herself in public, and lastly how she behaves in private.

> *"Elegance is not about being noticed, it's about being remembered."*
>
> —*Giorgio Armani*

A Ladylike Personality. When a woman behaves like a lady, she will always take responsibility for herself and her mistakes. You should never blame someone else for the things that don't go in your favor. You are in control of the level of happiness you reach. When she knows what she wants, she will do whatever it requires to get it done; within reason. A lady always has manners. She knows how to respect others, and she demands respect. She will always say "please" and "thank you." When she hurts someone, she will make an effort to apologize. She is humble, and she is always genuinely grateful for everything someone does for her.

A lady can accept all of her flaws. She understands that things will not always go her way and when a problem presents itself, she handles it with grace. A lady is capable of working with the hand that she was dealt. She will never allow herself to sit around depressed and sulk in her misery. A lady will never use her energy giving attention to people and situations that are undeserving of it. She never concerns herself with the unimportant things. A lady is very generous with her time. She will also lend her resources to those in need. She is always looking forward to the future and maintains a positive outlook on life. She is consistent with encouraging others to be more ladylike. A lady will always want to continue learning. She will never miss an opportunity to learn something new. She will never compare herself to others, nor will she try to compete with another woman. She will always acknowledge and accept her strengths as well as her weaknesses. A lady will always have an adamant work ethic. She will always go above and beyond to maintain order in her life.

A Lady in Relationships. When it comes to in relationships, she is always loyal to her significant other. A lady will never speak negatively about her companion in public, but instead, she'll praise the person she's dating. A lady knows what goes on between two people should stay between those two individuals. A lady knows how to control her anger. If something upsets her, she'll never take it out on everyone else. She is always polite and trustworthy. She is always patient and caring towards children; she would never let them go uncomforted. A lady will always act with maturity, and she will never treat someone in a way that makes them feel less than. A lady will never consistently nag her significant other, even if the person isn't doing what she feels should be done. A lady will be independent. She will always appear calm, responsible and mature. A lady will stay in control of her future, and she will never put it in the hands of someone else.

A Ladylike Appearance. A lady will always take care of herself. Her looks will always be important to her. She will make sure she maintains her health, and will always eat and exercise properly. A lady will always remain poised in any situation. A lady will never sacrifice her reputation to impress anyone. She will always dress appropriately. A lady doesn't mind sacrificing a little bit of comfort to look her best. She will always represent her significant other in the best way possible.

> *"You cannot act like flip flops and expect to be treated like Louboutins."*
>
> *—Unknown*

A Lady in Public. A lady will never air out her dirty laundry in public. She is always attentive when necessary, she is a great listener, and all always has a pleasant conversation. Things with her are never one-sided and all about her. A lady will deal with her problems privately. She also won't sit around male bashing with her friends. A lady will maintain the behavior that will make it easy for her love interest to take her home to meet their family. She will always dress for the occasion. A lady will never lead a person on intentionally. If she isn't interested, she would never pretend as if she is. She knows her place in a relationship and would make the person she's dating proud to hold her hand in public. A lady will never accept gifts without showing her gratitude, and she will never accept a gift if there is an expectation of something in return. A lady will never raise her voice or use profanity in public. She will express her opinion when she has something to say. If there is a disagreement, she can speak without drawing attention to the discussion. A lady can have an intelligent conversation with other intellectual people and remain comfortable. A lady will always speak clearly and precise. She isn't violent unless she is forced into a situation to defend herself. She will protect her family and her friends the same way she will protect herself. A lady is always capable of displaying humility even when she feels the situation warrants a different display of emotions. She will accept praise for her accomplishments without demanding more attention than is needed. A lady doesn't feel the need to brag and boast. She let's all of her accomplishments speak for themselves.

A Lady In Private. A lady will always make a house a home. She will work non-stop to make sure the living space is very comfortable. A lady will keep her house clean, and she will try hard to be the perfect hostess for guests. A lady will always avoid discussions filled with gossip and rumors.

While some women may disagree with some of the points below, some general factors will demonstrate lady like behavior. It is important to carry these practices wherever you are. For some, it may not be important to be admired. For others, it is a requirement. We should be very mindful of the impressions we give to other people, primarily the first impression. Many people have met someone and become less interested because of their actions. You will most likely remember your first meeting with someone, especially if it wasn't a good one. If you want it to be memorable in a good way, make sure that it is a positive experience.

Social Manners. A lady should always practice common everyday etiquette. This means you should understand certain rules. When it comes to social manners, you should never dwell on a person's mistakes. You can't change the past, so it's best to move on. A lady should always know how to conduct herself in social environments. When you head out to a restaurant, make sure you have your dining etiquette intact. You should never act classless and embarrass yourself or the people you are dining with. You should know which cutlery is appropriate. If your waiter or waitress has demonstrated great service, be sure to leave a tip. A tip is earned and not given, so reward them for a job well done.

As independent women, we are accustomed to taking care of everything ourselves. Because of this, when we are involved with someone, and they want to help, we tend to continue doing things for ourselves. A lady should make the person she's dating feel useful. Even though you are fully capable of performing the task, you should let the person take care of it. Even something as simple as holding the door for you. You could hurt their feelings and make them feel unwanted by denying their assistance. A lady should always try her hardest to maintain a positive attitude, especially in a social setting. You will need to learn how to express your anger or discomfort without making a scene in public. By no means do you want to be known as a drama queen. This could have you disinvited to social events.

"Keep your heels, head and standards high."

—*Coco Chanel*

Ladylike Job Etiquette. A lady is always capable of being a team player. There will always be someone that may get on your nerves. Maybe they don't work as hard as you and they aren't pulling their weight. Unless you are the boss, it isn't your place to reprimand them and tell them what they are doing wrong causing a big scene. You should always show patience. If for some reason you run into a situation where you don't know how to do something, you should take the time to learn. There are things about us all that could be improved. In your head, you may think you are perfect. Trust me; there is always something that you could do better. You should never be afraid of learning. Many people in the world will never have the opportunity to improve, so you should never take learning for granted. There are some things you should always make a priority. This includes respecting yourself and others in the workplace. There is never a reason to speak condescendingly to someone. Even if you have more knowledge than them or you are in a higher position. There is never need to talk to an adult as if they are a child. A lady should always look the person in their eyes when having a conversation and give them her undivided attention.

Just as there are instances that make a woman ladylike, there are instances that don't. In today's time, popular trends and a lack of guidance make it hard for our youth to find good examples. There are many ways that women make it difficult for themselves. If you don't present yourself as a lady, you can't expect to be treated like one. Some women don't see their inappropriate behaviors as an issue, so they don't feel the need to address them. If you want to be seen in a better light, then there are some behaviors that you must learn to eliminate. Nowadays, women seem to accept degrading themselves and one another. We should never tolerate disrespect and under no circumstance should we disrespect ourselves. Instead of labeling ourselves as 'good women,' we're out here telling the world that we are 'bad b*#ches.' For the life of me, I will never understand why a woman would want to be addressed as any kind of b*#ch. Regardless of the word that you put in front of it, the negative connotation still exists. There is nothing about that title that shows your strength or your self-worth. It doesn't show your level of intelligence either. As a woman, you should look for a genuine person with morals and values that will respect you. A respectable person who appreciates a classy woman would never look for a bad b*#ch nor would they pursue a real relationship with one.

You have to figure out if you are comfortable with being nothing more than a sex object to the other person or if you want to be something much more. Respecting yourself goes a very long way. You can demand that others respect you when you have ladylike behavior. Another behavior that can be a complete turnoff is the unnecessary use of profanity. Even if you are in the comfort of your home, it is still unladylike behavior. You show your lack of vocabulary by regularly using profanity. In social settings, you should avoid it because you can give people the wrong impression. Women who constantly speak in this manner appear uneducated and unable to converse with basic verbiage.

The next one on the list is engaging in physically confrontations with each other. There are many instances where women fight each other. Mostly, for reasons that aren't even worth the time or energy. It certainly isn't worth damaging your reputation. What type of example does that show our youth? A lady should be able to resolve conflict without the use of her hands. Classy women know they need to be a great example at all times. They realize you never know who is watching with plans of following in your footsteps. Teaching our youth better conflict resolution is important. It is also a need to show your peers this as well. Sure, you've heard the quote, "birds of a feather flock together." You would never want your reputation to be damaged because of the way your friend has behaved. There is nothing worse than being attached to something that has nothing to do with you. Many people are serving prison sentences right now because of a crime their friends committed. You should be very careful of those you choose to call your friends. If they act inappropriately in public, it is probably best to be their associate from a distance. This may lower the risk of being guilty by association. If you have to fight over someone, then that person isn't the one for you. You should keep it classy and move on with your life.

Next on the list is women that constantly want to be on the scene. Yes, when you are younger you want to see the world. You want to party as much as you can and live your life as an adult. Having fun is fine. The problem with always partying is it can do some things to your reputation and your health. It may seem cool to bounce from one night club to the other. To dress scantily clad and take tons of inappropriate photos. As a young adult, it may seem cool to have one night stands or sleep around with multiple men. The problem is being young isn't an excuse for recklessness. You could make one choice that could alter your future in a negative way for the rest of your life. Many times the consequence doesn't seem to match the deed. You'll meet tons of fun people while you're out drinking all the time. It's not likely you'll meet someone worth getting to know better. Even if you don't have plans on being a wife and a mother, you should still want to keep your reputation intact. If you choose this lifestyle, you can't complain later on when all your friends are in relationships, and you're still single. You cannot change the past. Therefore, you may not ever be able to modify the way people look at you once you have continuously shown them this side.

Another issue that prevents women from being seen as classy is caring about their physical appearance more than their actions. You could be wearing the most expensive clothes, but your attitude can make you look cheap. What you are wearing won't matter if no one can deal with your attitude. You aren't only considered classy because of your clothing. You have to have the complete package and emit a ladylike attitude to be respected as such. Women also have a tendency to compare their relationships to that of their friends or people on television. We see relationships that look great in public, and we assume that things are the same way in private. The reality is, that is rarely the case. Some people have become good at pretending or putting on a show. This is a false representation of a real relationship. Have you been that friend looking at others that are far from classy; yet, they have a stable relationship before you do? So, does that mean they are doing something right? Maybe, but that doesn't mean everything you are doing is wrong either. This could be the time you need to work on yourself. Start preparing for something greater. So don't give up! Your time is coming but first, work on you.

"A guy wants a classy girl who is smart and has goals - someone that he wouldn't be afraid to bring home to his parents."

—*Victoria Justice*

Moving on to the next subject, which lists the reasons why some women are still single. If it is your intention to remain single then, by all means, do what's best for you. However, if you ever want to be in a serious relationship, you will need to address some of the behaviors that make it difficult to take things to the next level. Some people will argue the way they were raised makes the difference. For example, some people feel that African American women aren't raised to be submissive to their significant other, unlike other ethnic groups. Now, we're not saying this doesn't happen in some African American relationships. Sure, there are many single mothers and most times their daughters grow up with them not being in a relationship. We are a product of our environment, but that doesn't mean that we can't change this stereotype. You have the ability to improve areas of your personality and behavior that aren't appealing or deemed classy.

One issue is that some women are so used to being single, they don't know what it is like to have someone expect certain things from them. Because they are single, they may not be able to share their emotions with someone effortlessly. Essentially, they become emotionally detached and self-supportive. People say they want a strong independent woman, but once they're involved with one, it's a lot of work. When you are in a relationship, it is important that you use your ladylike personality. You no longer have to take care of everything and now have to share your emotions. You have to learn how to remove yourself as the boss and become a partner. A woman that wants to play both roles in a relationship can sabotage it unknowingly. You have to allow yourself to be vulnerable with your emotions, feelings, and trust. This is the time that you can lay back, relax and let someone take care of you for once. Being in control and bossy isn't necessary anymore once you have someone by your side. So, sit back, relax and allow yourself to be pampered.

Another unfavorable trait is a woman who only cares about themselves and their desires. You never want to appear selfish. It isn't conducive to any relationship, and most likely things will fall apart before you know it. Then, you'll be sitting there trying to figure out why things didn't work out. No one wants to spend time without someone who acts as if there is a disconnect with the person they are dating. No relationship can survive that way. Be open to the needs of others, or you may find yourself alone for a very long time. Balance is necessary. Listen to others the same way they listen to you. Being unable to hear a person's side or unable to communicate isn't ladylike behavior. A lady makes sure she listens before she speaks to understand and gives the respect she demands.

As a lady, there is another behavior that you should be aware of, which is being extremely picky. Now, of course, I would never recommend that you just take whatever is available and accept less than you deserve. I'm not saying that at all, but you shouldn't be so selective that you miss out on something good. Whether you agree or not; this could be seen as a prejudice. The layman's definition of prejudice is to have a predisposition of. Some women can be uninterested in a person for a multitude of reasons before getting to know them. If the person doesn't look a certain way, then they're not given a chance. I understand beauty is in the eye of the beholder. Does this mean they aren't a great person, though? No, it doesn't. In addition to this, some women often don't have patience for the subtle approach. They'll say the person is too soft and not aggressive enough. These days, people base their attractions strictly by physical appearances, stylish clothing, and automobiles. If the individual has the eye-catching materials, then they appear to be the best candidate. In reality, this a widespread misconception. Their style or the type of vehicle they drive have nothing to do with the amount of money they make or how successful they may be. You can't determine a person's bank account balance by the type of shoes they are wearing. Truthfully, the ones that are flaunting and profiling rarely make the most money. Having this sort of superficial mentality could make you less approachable. People talk, and you'll most likely be labeled as shallow, selfish, and conceited amongst other derogatory names. This doesn't mean you need to get involved with someone you feel isn't attractive. It means you shouldn't be inconsiderate or tactless about it. A lady knows how to reply appropriately, how to decline gracefully and never leave someone feeling bitter or embarrassed.

"She is clothed with strength and dignity, and she laughs without fear of the future."

—Proverbs 31:25

The next topic is the fact that some women expect to be with that special someone, but aren't deserving of one. Some women don't possess the qualities they're demanding a person bring to the relationship. Many people set all of these standards as if what they have to offer is better than everyone else's. Some women have a long list of unrealistic expectations. Meanwhile, they haven't done any work to better themselves. Some women are more attracted to a person that constantly splurges on designer clothes, jewelry, and fancy automobiles. They rather date that kind of person versus one who lives comfortably, has good credit and a savings account. Shockingly, this woman could be barely making ends meet. If you are looking for someone for the sole purpose of supporting you financially, you are seeking a 'parent' not a significant other.

We should never accept anything less than complete respect. This is non-negotiable. Someone that will hold open our doors or who will pull out our seat at the table. Chivalry isn't dead! We should expect more than late night escapades. The person trying to court you should work for your attention, so you have to raise the bar. Before you lay out a list of requirements, you should have achieved these things for yourself as well. Begin to care less about what they are wearing and care more about what's in their mind and hearts. You will be able to adjust the materialistic standard and focus more on the internal qualities that they may have. You can always change someone's style, but you can't always correct their character flaws. A lady should always keep these things in mind.

The next thing that isn't ladylike is only depending on your looks. If you want to find a decent person to date, you'll need to have brains to compliment your beauty. I agree it's important to have a good appearance. A lady should always make sure she looks presentable. You should want to look your best, but you should not lean on your looks as the foundation of who you are as a person.

Your looks will only get you so far, and eventually, as you age your looks will fade. If you don't have anything else to rely on you could be denying yourself happiness with a companion, growth, and success.

The last issue that isn't becoming of a lady is the inability to forgive. Attitude is everything, especially when going into a new relationship. Many of us have been hurt in past relationships. Unfortunately, we hold on to those situations and bring the energy into the next one. A lady is capable of treating each person accordingly. She should be in control of her feelings, and this includes being able to forgive. You don't have to forget, but you shouldn't punish one person for something someone did in the past. If you are carrying baggage into a new relationship, I can almost guarantee it won't last long. Many times, we sabotage our friendships and relationships. If you are the common denominator in all of the problems, the issues lie within you. Some of us are addicted to drama, and it is nothing ladylike or classy about that. If you enjoy watching other women gradually increase their success, and you are content with being idle; it may be time for some self-reflecting. It's important to look within yourself and be brutally honest. For the most part, if you are exhibiting ladylike behavior, you'll find that life flows better than women who don't. You'll be a lot happier because there's a lot less stress. Life won't be perfect, but you'll be better prepared for the pitfalls. It took a very long time for me to become comfortable with doing some self-evaluation without being overwhelmed with emotions. The ability to accept your flaws comes with maturity. You should always be your worst critic and your biggest cheerleader.

There is no need to feel guilty about your past behaviors because each day you wake up is another opportunity to change and make a difference. You can look at it as a rebirth; a way to say "goodbye" to your negative past, and "hello" to a positive future. If possible, it would be great if you get an accountability partner; someone you can trust who is experiencing the same issues. Making a total life change is very tough. There will be times you will want to give up and revert to your old ways. There will also be times when your accountability partner may feel the same way.

When you rehash your past mistakes, it could make you depressed if you allow them to consume you. If this happens, it's not the end of the world, so don't panic. You are human, and sometimes we have uncontrollable feelings. Truthfully, you will never stop thinking about your past mistakes. The goal is to think about them less and less. You should want to live a life where you don't have regrets. You should look at your mistakes as lessons you've learned. You aren't always going to get what you want because it may not be for you. I am a firm believer in 'whatever is meant for you will be received.' So, never cry over spilled milk. Grab another gallon, fill your glass to the brim and take a sip. Take it one day at a time and don't pressure yourself to change overnight. When you look back on your life at how far you've come, you'll feel blessed and pleased with the results. You'll be proud of the new you. You will be an example and a role model for other people. You will be the woman that everyone is proud of, and all want to become. This feeling is unexplainable. The day you experience this; will be one of the best days of your life.

"A girl should be two things, classy and fabulous."

—*Coco Chanel*

Social Conduct / Social Interaction

When speaking of social conduct, there are often many misunderstandings. There are certain behaviors that society deems acceptable, and somehow we are all led to believe we should accept what society says. Depending on your culture, you may view things differently. There will be many behaviors that are allowed in some places that just aren't in others. We could debate for days about who a woman should be and what a woman should do. However, there will never be one particular model that every person follows. Fortunately, every woman is very different. Even if we share the same ethnicity, the same culture, or originate from the same region; we still won't have the morals, values, and beliefs.

We are influenced by our family, friends, teachers, television, and social media. In addition, many other aspects of our lives push us in one direction or another. Behavior is also often shaped by those we admire, what we perceive as beautiful and what we categorize as successful. When you think of social conduct, you think of the way an individual behaves in public. It can be how you conduct yourself at a social event or a post to your social media page. We all have a vision of how we think a woman should behave. You should always publicly act in a manner that doesn't damage your reputation to the point where it becomes unfixable. It is very difficult to get people to forget. Some things will be etched in their minds forever regardless of how you conduct yourself afterward.

So what are these standards or codes of conduct? We have compiled a list of ethics on which we feel clarity is needed to help women understand the importance of the way we conduct ourselves socially.

Sometimes we go through things in life we have trouble overcoming. It could be a breakup with a companion or stress at work that may cause us to make unhealthy choices and bad decisions. Whenever you react off pure emotion without taking the time to think matters over, you will most likely mishandle the situation. It is important that you always respond to a situation with your brain and heart. Make decisions based on what you know and not solely on how you feel. If you find you are unable to do so, it is always best to have a friend who you can rely on for help.

It never hurts to have someone who knows you almost as good as you know yourself. This person shouldn't be one to judge you. Instead, they should be there for you, even if it's only to lend a listening ear. You should never confide in someone you can't trust. It doesn't make sense to feel worse than you did before speaking to them. This person should be there to guide you in the right direction whenever your vision gets a little cloudy. If you aren't thinking clearly, you want someone around whose opinion you can undoubtedly trust. Someone who genuinely has your best interest at heart. You need to be able to depend on them to help you avoid making a decision that may place you in a worse predicament. If there is a female or even a group of women you dislike; don't give them the power to have control of your emotions. Especially, if this is someone you may have been friends with at some point in time. You never want to infuriate someone that knows your deepest darkest secrets because they will not hesitate to divulge them to the world once you've pissed them off. This could cause a world of drama for you and your associates.

We are all guilty of talking negatively about people for whatever reason with the hopes of them never finding out what has been said. Sadly, the majority of the things you don't want people to know somehow finds its way to the surface. So, in most situations, it is best to keep your opinions to yourself. Some things just don't need to be said. There would be less conflict in the world if more people learned how not to speak their minds in every situation. You'll be surprised at how much information comes to light in the midst of a heated discussion. You could learn things that may have been said about you years prior. You have to be wise enough to know when someone is telling you something because they care about your well-being or if their intent is to start drama. Once you figure that out, you will learn a valuable lesson in 'weeding out the real from the fake.'

For example, when it comes to starting drama, immature people often pick out everything they determine wrong with another woman's outfit, hair or makeup. It is elementary for trouble makers to whisper to their friends about the next girl across the room. Many people make themselves feel better about their insecurities by tearing down another person. Delving further, we have noticed an outfit our friend is wearing isn't presentable, yet we didn't say a word. It's almost as if we feel like we have one up on the person that doesn't have it all together. We shouldn't have an issue with telling our friends they are improperly dressed. We should also have a discreet way to let them know there is an issue. We shouldn't make it obvious and draw more attention by saying it in front of someone or yelling it across the room. We have to learn that there are simple ways to convey this information without the need to let everyone else know. It can be incredibly embarrassing for your friend. Don't be that type of person to someone you call a friend. You can also let a stranger know there is something out of place. As long as it is genuine and not a condescending comment. It may surprise you, but that person will most likely be very grateful and appreciative of it.

Another code of social conduct involves your circle of friends and who their enemies or rivals may be. There are always those friends who feel you need to dislike someone because they do. In the real world, this is harder than it sounds. It could be your co-worker that doesn't like another co-worker. Since you are close friends with one of them, you're expected not to interact with the other one. This could be awkward since you have to see them for eight hours a day. This is ridiculous and unrealistic. As silly as it sounds, many people think this way. They feel as though your loyalty lies in believing in whatever they deem right. Now, there are some situations where this is understandable. Maybe that person has done something that has also affected you negatively. In your case, you were able to be the bigger person and forgive them. However, your friend hasn't found it in her heart to get passed it. This will cause a dilemma because they will expect you to follow suit. You are more mature and able to move on from situations that don't have a detrimental effect on your life. You should never feel the need to be childish because someone else is. You should want to represent yourself in a mature adult manner at all times. There are ways to deal with conflict that doesn't involve someone getting upset with their friend for speaking to their 'enemy.' Everyone has to grow up and move on. It is impossible to avoid every person your friend dislikes. If you go through life that way, you will end up losing on both ends.

People have the tendency to be very mean to one another for no reason at all. Some are even bullies and exhibit hate towards complete strangers. Sure, this is very immature behavior. Some people will be malicious towards others no matter what. These actions probably make them feel better about themselves and their shortcomings. Maybe as a child, they went through a period where they were treated the same way. This may have sparked their need to display these actions. Either way, most people who behave this way are 'hurt people who hurt people.' On the other hand, some people are just 'keeping it real.' They want, to be honest at all times even if it's saying what people don't want to hear. This doesn't make them a bad person. It just means they feel honesty is always better than lying to someone. Nonetheless, it may still make the person on the receiving end feel the same. What matters most, is it coming from an honest place without any ill intent to harm you or diminish your self-esteem.

We've all been at a social event and snapped a bunch of pictures with a group of friends. Maybe you weren't looking your best in some of the photos. The phone used to take the pictures belonged to your friend who looked amazing in every shot. Unfortunately, you feel you look terrible, and you're not pleased. You're so unhappy; you tell your friend not to post any of the pictures. If this friend disregards what you've said and shares the photos on social media anyway; then you may need to evaluate your friendship. I would not be too happy if my friend posted a photo of me I didn't like. Especially, after voicing my concern to her in advance. You shouldn't do this to a friend or anyone for that matter. This could hurt someone's self-esteem and ruin a friendship. We all have to be mindful and considerate when dealing with our friends, their feelings, and similar situations.

An additional code of social conduct is dealing with someone your friend may be interested in dating or have dated in the past. Many people will say if you weren't dating the person then it shouldn't even matter. That notion is just as bad because your friend has told you she is interested in the person. Maybe she hasn't had enough nerve to approach the person, or maybe she doesn't think she is on their level. Regardless, because she hasn't taken the approach doesn't mean the person is 'fair game.' You aren't a good friend if you were aware of her feelings and still made the selfish decision to pursue the person. A good friend would never intentionally do something like that. Now, if she has dealt with the person in the past, it's not even an option for you to date them. It doesn't even matter if their situation amounted to nothing more than a one night stand. The person is still off limits to you. If you are very close friends, you probably know almost everything about her sexual past. Maybe she had some risky behavior in the past you thought was unsafe. You may even know the number of her sexual partners of which you disapprove. If this is the case, you should be profoundly uncomfortable having sex with someone after her. You don't know the sexual history of her partners and many people practice unprotected sex. If that isn't enough to deter you, then nothing else probably will.

One more code as it relates to friends and their relationships is you should never remain silent when you know your friend is falling for someone unworthy of her time. I know, you can't make an adult listen or do something they don't want to do. Because of that, there's a possibility she won't be receptive to this and may even think you are a little jealous. She may even believe you want the person for yourself or you just don't want her to be happy. In this instance, it's perfectly fine to step back and let her make the decision on her own. You can let her know you were only giving her this information as a friend and you understand she is capable of doing what she feels is best. You could also let her know regardless of the outcome you will still support her and be there if she needs you. You should never let anything like this ruin a friendship. There have been many occasions where friendships have been torn apart for similar reasons. What you're doing is the right thing. Look out for your friend since you feel there will be an adverse outcome. But as the adage says, "you can lead a horse to water, but you can't make him drink." All you can do is offer the information, but you can't force her to take heed.

There is the touchy topic which deals with the social conduct of women. Many of us may have or had a friend involved with a person who was married or in a relationship. Some people encourage their friends to continue their relationship with the individual. Even if you aren't married, you should have an understanding of the proper way to conduct yourself as a wife. It is never acceptable to be involved with someone who is married or in a relationship. As a friend, you should be concerned with her behavior and question her level of trust. If she is willing to deal with another person's wife or husband; what makes you think she won't do the same to you? Clearly, she doesn't have any morals or values. Most importantly, in her eyes, marriage isn't a sacred bond. For those reasons, this isn't someone I would feel comfortable having around the person I'm dating. For argument's sake, let's change the scenario and pretend she's married and has limits to what she will and won't do. Maybe she only steps outside of her marriage when there are issues at home. Other than that, she's a decent wife. Regardless of the reason, it's still wrong and unacceptable behavior. Not being one to judge, but I think she's making excuses to justify her wrongful actions. If this were my friend, I wouldn't trust her any longer, and our friendship would suffer. Ultimately, we would no longer be friends. If she could be disloyal to the one person she vowed her life to; for me, it wouldn't be any different.

As women, we are very critical of ourselves. We may have a disdain for certain things about our appearance. We can look into the mirror at any given time and identify multiple things we see as flaws. In reality, most people will never see everything you see wrong with yourself. In fact, they will tell you the truth, which is you are the most beautiful woman they have ever seen. Sadly, even with that compliment, you may still say something negative about yourself. As a friend, we should never encourage this kind of behavior. If your friend says she is overweight, you should give your support and tell her she is fine just the way she is. Now, if you agree, you shouldn't pacify her. Instead of lying or merely confirming her thoughts, you should help her lose weight. You could start by going to the gym with her and even eating healthier foods together. You should never make her feel insecure because that will only compound her current issues. Her weight could be detrimental to her health, so it isn't helpful to make her feel any worse about herself than she already does.

Something else we should avoid is addressing each other with inappropriate names. If your name isn't b*#ch on your birth certificate, you should not allow anyone to address you as one. It's sad that some women think addressing each other with derogatory names is a sign of endearment. The irony is, some people allow their friends to call them out of their name with no recourse. Strangely enough, they become enraged when someone outside of their circle calls them the same name. Why is it acceptable for your friends to address you in that manner, but not for anyone else? If the word is unacceptable from one set group of people, then it needs to be unacceptable for everyone else. The word isn't a juxtaposition and has a negative connotation regardless of who's using it to address you. You must remember that you can't demand respect from one person, but allow other people to be disrespectful towards you. There are certain names you should never use when referring to friends and family. You should treat people with respect, so respect is reciprocated.

Sometimes we have a tendency to over think situations and take them personally. In some cases, we allow our minds to make us believe there is a problem when there isn't one. We also feel the need to discuss things during the most inopportune times. We should be close enough with our friends to come together when there is a problem or miscommunication. There's no need to let the ill feelings fester only to bring them up later.

Sometimes, a person could be upset about something that has nothing to do with you. Instead of assuming it's about you, approach them as a concerned friend trying to figure out the issue. If they choose not to let you know what their problem is, you should move on. You have to trust that if and when they are ready to discuss it with you, they will.

We should value our friends, and we should always be able to come to one another and settle our differences. Some friendships have ended over a simple lack of communication. Some people have tremendous difficulty expressing themselves. Many people hold their feelings inside to avoid having a verbal or physical confrontation. There isn't an issue with having feelings about a particular issue. You are entitled to feel the way you desire. There should never be a point where you feel you can't express your feelings because someone doesn't share the same consensus. We should never let a minor issue get out of control. It's all in your approach and delivery. Maybe use a softer tone or word things differently, so your words don't seem abrasive. This could avoid making the other person defensive. If not, neither person will be heard, and an argument will happen. If both people are upset and yelling at one another, tempers begin to flare, and the situation will rapidly escalate. Two friends should be able to sit down and have an actual conversation where one person speaks, and the other one listens without interrupting.

When it comes to advice, we are sometimes guilty of thinking we know it all. Regardless of the topic, at some point, we believe we are experts and qualified to tell someone else how to live their life. Because our suggestions are genuine and sincere, we are convinced we have the answers. We may have at one point or another, 'threw stones while living in a glass house.' We will swear up and down we know what a perfect relationship is when ours is in shambles. We sometimes give our opinions when they aren't requested, and this could cause a lot of friction in friendships. No one wants to be looked at as less than intelligent. We all make questionable decisions from time to time, and we shouldn't be crucified for it; especially by our friends. Giving advice is fine. Sometimes it's good to have an outside opinion, but we should never perceive it to be finite. You can have your opinion and choose not to agree. Two people will never have the same feelings for every situation. So, if your friend is telling you about a situation and asks for your advice, by all means, tell her your perspective and how you feel about it. Don't offend her by preaching and talking down to her. You should encourage her and let her know there may be other alternative ways to approach the situation. You can also assure her that you'll be in her corner unconditionally. Everyone needs a friend's support. We don't need friends who believe their ideals and principles are the beginning and end.

Now, let's address style. We should all have an overall style. You never want to be a carbon copy of someone else, including your family and friends. We are all unique, and we should always present ourselves with our best version of us. It is nerve-racking for someone to accuse you of imitating their style or their friend's style. Never mimic your friends. Even if you like something they're wearing, you can't expect it to look the same on you. Besides, let them have their moment, even if you feel it will look better on you. It is never a good idea to adapt someone else's style, over your own. You are a trendsetter, not a trend follower.

One important social code of conduct is the 'come together leave together' motto. Some women will hang out in the club with their friends, and once they meet someone, they are quick to ditch them and leave with the stranger. I have never been a fan of this because you never know what might happen once you're alone with the person. There have been times where my group of friends arrived at an event together, but by the end of the night, our group of five turned into a group of three. Then, you feel overly obligated to check on them and make sure they haven't left the club with a serial killer.

Your safety must always be number one! How would you feel if you awakened to the morning news detailing a story of your friend being murdered? This is not an exaggeration, and it could easily happen if we're not careful. Many people have experienced that horrific moment happen to their friend or loved one. Despite it happening daily, people are still entrusting their lives in the hands of strangers. I am a firm believer in, arriving together as a group and leaving together as a group. I could care less how much you lust over, or you're attracted to this person. My only concern is that you get home safely. So, if I have to drag you to my vehicle and have you pissed at me the following day; so be it. At least, you will be alive, and that is most important. Always keep your friends close because we live in a very dangerous world.

GIRL CODE

Another social code of conduct is never to let your friends become too intoxicated. Not only is this embarrassing, but it is also life threatening. A person is killed in an alcohol-related accident every fifty-three minutes. Even with the statistics as a matter of public record, many people still party, drink and drive home drunk. You'll drive with the windows down hoping the cool air keeps you awake. You sit up close on the steering wheel with both hands hoping this will help you focus and avoid crashing your car. How many of us have watched our drunk friend climb into their vehicle and wave goodbye to them? You knew they were extremely intoxicated, but you didn't make any attempts to stop them from driving off. They would be lucky only to get pulled over by the police. They could easily end up in a car accident; killing themselves or someone else. There should always be a responsible designated driver when you're out consuming alcohol. If no one in the group is sober, your next best option is getting home by taxi. There are so many lives that have been lost because people were selfish and decided to operate a vehicle under the influence. Unfortunately, this could be the one time you underestimate your level of intoxication, and you're unable to control the car. It is always better to be safe than sorry. Real friends do not let friends drive drunk.

In the aspect of discussing social behavior; we should always represent ourselves in the best way possible. This includes our friend selection, choice of clothing, being respectful, demeanor in public, risky behavior in sexual encounters, and limits to alcohol consumption. In today's times, many people are anxious to pull out their cell phones to snap photos and record videos. You never know who will see you in public acting inappropriately. You don't want to have a job interview and lose out on securing the position because of an online video exposing your lewd behavior. It's always important to be mindful of how your present actions could negatively impact you in the future. No one knows what the future may bring, but it's one less worry if you always conduct yourself as a lady.

You should be aware of your surroundings and never put yourself in any situations that could risk your life. If you fall short of that, your friends are supposed to step in and make sure you're safe. Your circle of friends should depend on each other to be there. You don't want a friend who is willing to degrade you to make them look or feel better. You also don't want a friend who wouldn't let you know you're embarrassing yourself and your actions are getting out of hand. Don't talk behind your friend's back and always keep their secrets to yourself. As a confidant, speaking to someone else about information that was entrusted to you, is disloyal and runs the risk of rumors being spread about the person.

You want always to be there and lend an ear and a shoulder to cry on in a time of need. Know when it is time only to listen and not voice your opinion. Sometimes, it is best to keep your opinion to yourself and avoid bashing someone because they made a decision you may not agree is acceptable. To be a great friend, you have to give everything you want to receive in return. You can't expect someone to be a true friend to you if you're not a real friend to them. Learn to value your friends and appreciate their existence. Some people aren't lucky enough to have supportive friends, so have their backs no matter what.

None of us are perfect, and we all experience moments of weakness. We should be very honest with ourselves as well as our friends. There's no need to put on a front and hide the truth from each other just to be thought of as the 'good girl.' Honesty is the policy, so be transparent. Be able to take advice as readily as you give it. Some people need to experience things for themselves, so sometimes your words will fall on death ears. That's fine, so don't become discouraged and unsupportive of your friends because of it. That is just the way things are in the real world, and we shouldn't expect anything more or anything less.

Work hard at being a positive influence in the lives of your friends and family members. It's impossible always to do the right thing, but it's not impossible to make more good decisions than bad ones. As long as you enter situations with the right attitude and intentions, your results will work in your favor. You shouldn't feel as though you have to be untrue or unreal because that never helps anyone get further. The goal is to lead by example, be there for those who need you and encourage our young women to do the same in their friendships and relationships. See it as a way to help them become a better person. Assist them to grow to be the type of women that stands for something and will not sacrifice their morals and values to 'be cool' or 'fit in.' It is imperative to build other women up because many people love to tear them down. Be the best you can be and encourage others always to do the same.

Branding and Professionalism in Business Matters

For years women have fought to be seen as equals in the workplace. And while there remains progress to be made, today you can find women in top positions at corporations all over the world. Women are an integral part of the workforce and have been successful in their roles for decades. Other women have chosen success down the more traditional path of stay-at-home-mom; while many modern women work both inside and outside the home. Regardless of a women's chosen career, whether it be corporate, traditional or any combination of the two, it is imperative that we respect each other's decisions and accept that no one path is more valuable than the other.

All too often, women are pitted against each

other in regards to their career choices. Some are told they are less of a woman if they forsake motherhood for a profession, others are told they lack ambition if they choose motherhood; while those who choose both are told they can't possibly give the proper attention to either their family or jobs. The truth of the matter is that none of these opinions hold any truth. They are all just another way to draw any invisible line that divides three perfectly viable options for a woman's life. The choice as to which should always be left in the hands of the individual, while those on the outside should implore the 'to each its own' tactic. We should never be so concerned with what someone else is doing that we take the focus away from our careers, goals, and ambitions. You'd be surprised how far you can get by leaving the 'crabs in the barrel' mentality behind.

For those women who have chosen or will choose to pursue a career outside of the home, it important to have a firm grasp on professionalism and branding for success. As simplistic as they sound on the surface, both professionalism and branding play a significant role in your success or failure. We have compiled a simple, yet effective list of do's and don't's to provide a better understanding of how to achieve and maintain your desired career goals. First, we'll touch on the mistakes and bad habits that may prevent you from advancing up the corporate ladder.

If by some chance, you have found yourself at a point in your career where you feel you are being overlooked for advancement opportunities, then it may be time for a little self-evaluation. While biases and other factors beyond our control occasionally have an effect, it's safe to say that sometimes the fault lies in our behavior. It's quite easy to pass off bad behavior as 'just a mistake' and to pretend as if it is no big deal. Besides, we're just 'keeping it real, right? It's just who you are, right? You shouldn't be expected to be anyone other than yourself, right? Wrong! Never, for any reason, should you undermine your professionalism with inappropriate behavior. Always appear poised and at your best, so no one has a reason to question your ability. The outside world is hard enough on you, without you actively contributing to your downfall or stagnation. Be sure to prevent sabotaging your career by avoiding the following behaviors:

- Often, we lack the confidence to forge

ahead. If you don't believe in yourself, you certainly can't expect anyone else to. If others around you sense a low-confidence level, it will almost immediately damage your credibility in the workplace. No one wants to put an employee in a higher position that isn't even sure they can perform at that level. Make sure you exude confidence, in your words and actions. You have to believe you are capable and can invaluably contribute to any situation.

• Poor body language can be damaging to a reputation. Is it always fair; no. Does the perception always match our real intentions and understanding; no. Does any of this actually matter; absolutely not. Your body language determines how those around you perceive you, and while it's not always correct, perception is reality. Poor body language can communicate a lack of confidence, unpreparedness, rudeness and defensiveness; all of which leave room for others to doubt your capabilities. When in a professional setting; it is imperative to always to be aware of your body language as it can make or break you. Unfortunately, 'breaking you' diminishes any chance of you moving up the corporate ladder.

- Never downplay your abilities or achievements. Contrary to what has been drilled into many of us, sometimes modesty is not the best policy. By not owning up to your accomplishments, you give others the right to ignore them as well. It's true that no one likes a braggart, but celebrating yourself and acknowledging the great things you have done is not bragging. Even if you haven't made it as far as you've liked, you should always be proud of yourself and hold your achievements in a positive light. Besides, if you don't, who will?

- Your personal feelings should never be the sole basis for a business decision. Always base your business dealings on your knowledge and experience, not your personal feelings. You're not a robot, and no one should expect you to be one, but business is business and personal is personal. Regardless of the position you hold, your purpose is to ultimately bring value to your employer, even if you're self-employed. By no means, should you ever ignore your gut feelings; but when it's decision-making time, make sure your choices are sound and fit into achieving success. This applies to workplace opinions as well. By their nature, opinions are often based more on personal feelings; therefore, it is easy for emotions to rise when debating an opinion vastly different from your own. In these cases, allow your experience and knowledge of your particular workplace environment to dictate your approach to discussing emotionally charged opinions.

• Never allow a disconnect between your appearance and ability. Even though there is no universal dress code, and the standard of professional dress varies by the office; you should always strive to dress professionally. Regardless if you work for someone else or if you are self-employed, you represent a brand during business hours. The visual image you put forth sends a message of professionalism and by association, depicts your ability. Proper workplace attire goes beyond remaining within the confines of professional dress. Ill-fitting clothing can spell disaster. Clothing that is too small can lead to you appearing fidgety and inattentive as you constantly adjust them to avoid the threat of a wardrobe malfunction. Clothing that is too baggy can make you look frumpy and less confident. As women, we have the right to dress as we please; of course, we do. But it's best to use our discretion when walking the fine line between free expression and professionalism. Why fit in when you were born to stand out; because it's in the best interest of your career. That's not to say that you have to look and dress like everyone else. Just look around and take cues from those around you to gauge the general tone of your workplace's attire. When planning your move up through the ranks, always remember to dress for the job you want, not the one you have.

- On no occasion should you ever be afraid of not being nice. Sometimes with women, the word nice is more than a 'four-letter-word.'

If we're too nice, we're pushovers; if we're not nice enough, we're b*#ches. The burden of being nice and the fear of being called a b*#ch often holds us back in the workplace. I'm not suggesting rude behavior that goes against basic common courtesy, but you have to realize there is a profound difference between being pleasant to be around and blindly appeasing everyone. You don't have to be everyone's best friend. Never apologize for having goals and doing what needs to be done to accomplish them. Say no to requests you don't want to meet, and don't feel bad about it. Step up, be a leader, if you so chose. Have standards for those you lead and have every expectation for those standards to be met. Be bold, stick to your principles and don't let anyone make you anything less than great for choosing you. Never sacrifice or stall your career ambitions for fear of being called names, because as the saying goes, "it's not what they call you, it's what you answer to."

- By no means should you ever compromise your character. We all have a set of guiding principles at our core that shape who we are. Never compromise your character. Hold on to it at all costs. When lines become blurry, and money or success is involved, it can be tempting to let character fall victim to advancement. Maintain your sense of integrity irrespective of who may or may not be watching.

• You should never neglect to show interest in your job. Those who are the most successful are typically go-getters who often display their drive. They usually go the extra mile and take any given opportunity to learn. When someone is focused on gaining success, it shows.

• Lacking proper communication skills is always an issue in the workplace. There are plenty of educated and intelligent people that haven't made it very far because they lack communication skills. No one will ever care about what you say when it has been voiced in an offensive way. It is critical in business to appear friendly and approachable. If there is an issue in the office, you should be able to communicate your issues without becoming belligerent. When it comes to communication, being average isn't where you want to be. No one is successful by merely being average. Depending on what field you work in you should also be able to communicate professionally with customers. A business will ultimately fail without customers, so you should have exceptional communication skills. You should always exceed the expectations of your employer.

- Don't let frustration cause you to act in a manner that you normally wouldn't. We all get frustrated at times, and it's okay, but what you can't do is let it affect your job performance. When we are overworked, it is easy to lose control. Instead of being poised and professional we appear weak, angry and frustrated. This is a terrible way to represent yourself in a professional environment. While most people will see a breakdown as a sign of weakness there is obviously and underlying situation that needs to be addressed. Frustration commonly occurs when a person feels trapped or at a standstill. If you find yourself feeling frustrated at work, you can do a few things to deal with it professionally. Sometimes the best thing for you to do is to take a step back and figure out why you are feeling frustrated before it spirals into anger. You never want to allow a little frustration to damage or end your career. It is important to learn to relax and try something new to keep frustration to a minimum. Don't harp on whatever it is that is bothering you; every situation provides a lesson that may help you in the future.

- Never hold onto anger. If for some reason frustration or anxiety leads to anger, it is time to get control of yourself. You never want your anger to breed a volatile work environment. One way to control bouts of anger is to recognize what your triggers are. If you learn to watch for the early signs, you can figure out a better way to manage your anger. As with any problem, the first step in correcting a problem is to realize that you have one. There will always be someone at work that you aren't very fond of. You may also come into contact with someone that is downright disrespectful. Two wrongs will never make a right, and you will run the risk of appearing unprofessional, not to mention possibly unstable or dangerous, if you aren't able to control yourself. You should always seek to resolve conflicts with as little drama as possible.

- Never allow personal issues to affect you in the workplace. Sometimes we carry problems from home into the workplace which could be a disaster. Be sure to keep your personal life and work life separate. If your goal is to maintain a professional image at work, focus on solving personal issues outside of the workplace before they do irreparable damage to your career.

With the popularity of social media, the importance of branding yourself, even if you are working for someone else, is paramount; especially in a professional setting. By creating an identifiable and respected brand, you can take control of how other's view you. Without doing so, you can become easily lost in the masses. You should be sure to take advantage of every opportunity to market yourself, to ensure that you stand out amongst the rest. Doing so could be the difference between being hired or not.

In many cases, your brand or reputation is all that you have. You never want your brand to be defined by bad choices and behavior, or by negative perceptions that others may have of you. Regardless of how you see yourself, you will be known by how others see you. If they associate you with negativity, mistakes, and unprofessionalism, then that is how you will be known; even if the qualities are the furthest from your real character.

When building your personal brand, you should remain consistent in your message across all boards ensuring that it represents the image you want to portray. If you are an expert on a particular topic or field, build a professional and personal brand that displays your talents and qualities to the fullest. Pay close attention to your interactions with your colleagues and study how those with direct knowledge of you receive your message. Your actions will always speak louder than words; therefore if your actions reflect your brand, others will soon notice. You need to ask yourself these questions: Do they genuinely connect you with the brand you claim? Do they respect your opinions on matters associated with your brand? If so, you are on the right path to building a strong, recognizable brand. If not, then it's back to the drawing board to refocus your efforts.

Even though your ego could be bruised in the process, a great way to learn what people perceive of you is to ask for feedback. It's always best to know your intention and how the perception of your attention have deviated from each other. The key is to be respected and clear on what you have to contribute. Ask yourself what your worth is and how it would compliment the success of the company. Most people truly aren't aware of what makes them different or what they have that makes them stand out. Your brand should be authentic, and all of the things that make you great at what you do should become a part of your personal brand. Spend some time learning what your strengths are as well as your passions and your goals. Seek feedback from those around you, being sure not just to ask your friends or those who may be more interested in sparing your feelings. When requesting feedback, ask for complete honesty and be prepared for responses that may make you uncomfortable. It will never benefit you if things are sugar coated to make you feel better. It will also be great to get this feedback from multiple sources.

Irrespective of your brand, its purpose is to establish you as the front-runner in your chosen field. You must have the necessary knowledge and proven skills to perform at the level you have branded yourself. Remain confident and focused, thereby demonstrating that your brand is worthy of support. You have to be prepared at all times to prove your worth and the value that your expertise and brand brings. Building a successful brand takes a lot of work and will not happen overnight. By putting in time and effort, your personal brand will soon come to fruition.

Once you've established your brand, you have to put forth the effort to support it and foster growth. Do not become complacent and allow your brand to become stale or stagnant. Without question, there will be times when your brand will need more work. That's not to say it will require a complete overhaul, but it will have to adapt to the ever-changing interest of the world around you.

When it comes to promoting your best qualities always keep in mind, there will never be anyone better than you. Therefore, self-promotion is always a must. Although you may eventually come to require the assistance of others, you should never solely rely on them for your promotional needs.

There are some tips for performing your absolute best in the workplace. As women, we believe in gender equality in our career fields. As long as we effectively do our jobs, we should expect equal pay and opportunities for promotions. We may have had success with doing things repetitiously, but it is a mistake to become comfortable with the routine. It is common to believe that if you display beneficial actions or positive behaviors, you will always gain success. This is true to an extent. To make it to the next level you need to apply your qualities to the equation. It takes more than a college degree or advanced college degree. Some may not attend college for many reasons, so it's important that you work hard and improve your skills to advance in your career. If not, there would be no need to offer you a promotion. You should be strategic in identifying what each benchmark requires then set your goals so that you can move up in position. Once you have a clear understanding of what is expected, you can begin implementing your plan. Executives put essential practices into their skill sets to become successful. You should be knowledgeable of the best practices for your ongoing plan.

Long-term planning is another practice, which could greatly assist with obtaining a promotion. We have all been asked where we see ourselves in a specific amount of years. Most of us randomly respond with the first thing that comes to mind. Going into your future unprepared can lead to exhaustion, lack of promotion or achievements. You could tirelessly work for years to no avail. When you look back on your career, you'll see there hasn't been any significant growth in your position. Many successful executives often set long-term goals for themselves. If you can visualize where you want to go, you can categorize the steps needed to get there. Even if it means accepting a job outside of your area of choice or expertise. Embrace this as an opportunity to gain knowledge and experience in a different area, which could be useful in the future. Never miss out on an opportunity to learn something new. It will be important to capitalize on your learning experiences and place them in your bank of knowledge for usage. You should never be comfortable with a lack of understanding on any subject. Once you have identified the key achievements you want to complete; the next step is to locate the resources you need to accomplish them.

The use of a mentor can also be a great asset to your brand and career. It is in your best interest to surround yourself with individuals that you can build ideas and discuss developmental plans. If you have the support of an influential mentor, you can increase your chances to advance positions sooner than expected. You shouldn't depend on someone else to help you find a mentor. If you focus on building a relationship with someone with similar experiences, they shouldn't have a problem with helping you achieve your short-term and long-term goals. Your mentor may not always be available, but you should be patient and understanding when it comes to someone using their personal time to assist you.

Networking is also a crucial step. If you take a look at successful people, they all participate in some degree of networking. You should always use networking to establish contact with others. This allows you the ability to gain information and access people who can be instrumental to your success. You should put a new strategy in place if your previous networking plan didn't work as anticipated. You must display your best qualities, so the prospective individual sees your value and ascertains if it's beneficial to work with you. This way there is established reciprocity rather than the sole need of the other person. Just as you may find someone to mentor and assist you; you could do the same for someone else. Once you commence working on new networking strategies, you should cross steps off your list.

You will also learn that your self-esteem if something else that can hinder your movements towards a promotion. If you are comfortable with self-promotion and you are confident and competent in a particular area, you will be able to use this to your advantage. You never want to overcompensate or be too aggressive, especially as a woman in a male-dominated workplace. This can do more harm than good. However, do not limit yourself because you're afraid of outperforming your male counterparts. If you find that you lack certain competencies, you will need to further your education in those areas. While some jobs offer education and training, it is your responsibility to locate opportunities for developmental growth.

The fact is, no one is perfect, and it's tough to progress believing otherwise. Sure, some self-absorbed people excel in business, but they too succumb to making mistakes along the way. You should never write down goals that are unrealistic or unattainable because you may set yourself up for failure. Never depend on luck to get you where you need to be. To be successful, you will have to work very hard because you get out what you put in. You can take some professional risks but in moderation. Be prepared to have setbacks and be tested at any time. You will need to eliminate self-doubt and stand firm on your abilities.

Invest time into knowing who you are, and maybe it will help mold the way others see you. When working with women that have succeeded in your field, look for a role model. Don't forget that you are a possible role model for someone else. Be conscious of this and remember you are being watched at all times, so always do your best. Your values should be just as consistent as your brand.

There is a belief that leaders are born and not made. I am a believer in the opposite because everyone can become a leader. Some people are more comfortable being in non-leadership positions. This does not constitute an inability to lead others. First, establish yourself then push your brand, so it evolves over time. Never rely on superficial characteristics and strive to receive the recognition you deserve. You want to keep in mind that; presumably, women leaders are held to much higher standards.

You should prepare yourself for the need to walk away. Some situations aren't worth holding on to because they are mentally and physically draining. There are times when a job can become so stressful that it begins to take its toll on you. If you ever find yourself in this situation, you have to evaluate all of the pros and cons. No matter the level of success you have or have not obtained, there is always the opportunity for better employment. If you realize this is the case, you want to advance and desire to work in a peaceful state of mind; it is probably best to look for a position at a different company.

It is an entirely viable option to walk away, and you should never feel like a failure because of it. In the end, it is much more important to walk into your place of employment without any anxiety or concerns. If you begin to dread going to work, it could be a sign that maybe the position isn't for you. Not every opportunity we are given will lead us to a better place. Ergo, it is best to take the needed time to figure out what is the best decision for your future.

Dating and Relationships

Regarding the topic of dating, many women find themselves confused and frustrated. We rarely understand why we feel this way. Maybe it could be we haven't had many good experiences. Somewhere along the line, we may have given up. With all of the dating apps and websites a click away, we tend to get comfortable hiding behind technology. We are comfortable saying things we may not say during a face to face encounter. Years ago, it was customary for women to be coy and allow gentlemen to make the initial contact. Even at a social event, men would approach and offer to buy us a drink or take us on a date. In recent times, things have drastically changed. Though many women may not be comfortable with being the pursuer, others don't mind it at all. Some men won't like a woman who comes on a little too strong. They can quickly lose interest because this could be perceived as a reversal of roles in a sense. Some men are still old fashioned and feel it's their duty to be a gentleman by allowing a woman to be herself. Some may be uncomfortable with a woman who chooses this approach, but others may be flattered.

It seems to be more acceptable to show forwardness inside of a dating app than it is in person. Some women are more aggressive in their modus operandi and feel the need to throw themselves at the person for attention. Most times, this will do the opposite of what it is you are trying to accomplish. You could give the wrong impression by displaying these types of actions and be perceived as being promiscuous. Unless that is the quality the person is seeking, more than likely they will be unattracted to your advances. Even if it is your nature to be aggressive, you may want to hold back a little. You should never want to give a person too much so soon. It could lower the chances of the relationship becoming successful. If you want to find an emotionally satisfying relationship at any point in your life, you have to make sure you focus on your worth and look for a person wanting the same.

It is imperative for you to change your values if you rather make yourself available for a person before getting to know them better. If you want someone to appreciate the qualities you have to offer, you have to make sure you equally value yourself. As a woman, we must value what God has given us and always represent ourselves with respect. We shouldn't be so eager to give ourselves to every person with whom we show interest. When you go through life bouncing from partner to partner, you lose certain virtues and self-respect. You would be appreciated more if you didn't make it so easy to be intimate with you. Even if this isn't how you usually handle the situation, it could be misconstrued because you are quickly offering yourself to the person.

While dating, you should be patient and get to know a person to determine if this is someone you are willing to give a chance. It is very easy to fall in lust if you only focus on the physical attraction and operate with your emotions. During this kind of experience, it is more of a sexual chemistry and less of what lies beneath the surface. You will see that most relationships with a foundation built on sex, aren't strong and don't have much longevity. Once sex is involved, we rarely take the time to learn additional things about the person. Your primary focus has now shifted to anticipate your next escapade. This is surely headed for disaster. If you aren't interested in getting to know someone, you shouldn't be willing to have casual sex with them either. If they're not worthy of your time then certainly they're not worthy of your body.

A woman should ultimately focus her attention on a person who is pursuing her for more than what she can offer in the bedroom. Many people are willing to suppress the sexual attraction between you two, so they can work on building something worthwhile. Even if you feel the urge to be sexually involved, let the person be respectful and not force the issue until they're ready to be intimate. As women, we are sometimes very impatient when it comes to what we want. This often causes us to want someone moving at our pace. You can ruin the situation before it begins if you make a person uncomfortable or feel forced into doing something they're not prepared to do. You are smart, so it won't take long to realize what you like and dislike about the person. Time is valuable, so don't waste it on someone you know has character flaws you're not willing to tolerate. But make sure you balance the pros and cons because there may be more great qualities than unfavorable ones.

We should always take responsible for the choices we make. If it results in a bad romance, then you have to live with that. If you don't assume the responsibility, you won't learn from your mistakes. This will hinder you from turning your life around. Subsequently, you run the risk of growing more frustrated with dating than you were before. When you embrace the ramifications, you will let go of any anger associated with your decisions and then look forward to a better dating situation in the future. Once you have found someone you are interested in, be yourself and take your time. It's not a race. You don't need to rush into anything without doing your due diligence. You will learn to make better choices and act responsibly.

Dating requires time, dedication, and communication. We all have made the mistake of opening up about everything that has happened in our previous relationship. There is absolutely no reason to divulge all of this information from the onset of a new situation. We shouldn't feel the need to tell a person everything at once. We all have experienced challenges in our relationships, but it is unhealthy to allow those instances to permeate a new relationship. It takes a lot of time get to know someone. Even after many years, there will be some things you still don't know about the person. If this person is interested in you, they will respect that you need to share information at your pace. Since you are a confident woman, you will find an eligible person ready to pursue you and be patient. Keep things honest and exciting because you need to have fun and highlight the happiness you'll have together in the future. Most people aren't interested in a woman they can walk over. I'm' not saying always be combative and argumentative, but stand up for herself. To have a positive dating experience, you have to be aware of the differences between the two of you. If we were all the same, dating would probably be a lot tougher for any of us. To help alleviate some of the trouble with dating, we have gathered some tips to make the process a little easier.

If you have a date set up, the anticipation could be very overwhelming. When meeting someone for the first time, always be prompt and on your best behavior; 'you never get a second chance to make a first impression.' You will, of course, want to look your best, but don't overdo it. Be classy, not trashy. What you wear will leave a lasting impression. Being on time is crucial because no one wants to feel like their time isn't valuable. By arriving on schedule, you show that you are courteous and dependable. Once you get there, be sure to make eye contact and avoid seeming unconcerned with what he is saying by constantly looking around the room. You should smile when it is appropriate, and you should engage in the conversation. This way, they won't feel as if they're engaged in a conversation with themselves. After the first date, you will know if you have any interests. If you don't, it is best to avoid taking things any further. A second date is pointless if you already know you don't want to go any further with the individual.

While on a date, it's important to avoid too much of 'playing it cool.' Find a balance, so you don't appear too eager or disinterested. Instead, you should focus on relaxing in the moment and being kind. Be yourself and allow your personality to shine. No one will enjoy the date if both of you are sitting there without much to say to each other. You should also pay close attention to the way you speak to each other. In the beginning, you don't know which topics may cause a heightened discussion. So, be conscious of your tone if the conversation becomes a bit emotional. It would behoove you to refrain from in-depth discussions about politics and religion, as these two topics are sure to ignite emotions with any disagreements. Sometimes, we are so headstrong in our beliefs; our tone can be offensive even when that isn't our intention. You have to hold an intelligent conversation without hurting the feelings of the other person. Avoid being loud and irate, so you don't embarrass the both of you. If this occurs, there may not be another date.

You should avoid asking your friends their opinions. In all actuality, what they think doesn't hold more value than how you feel. Since you and your friends are different, your preferences aren't the same. The final decision lies with you because you have to date the person. It is more important to build your relationship and learn about their qualities on your own, without the influence of what other people think. With dating and relationships, there isn't a magic answer or perfect formula for dating success. You have to be committed to the process, and in the event things don't go as planned, you have to decide if you're leaving or staying to come to some resolve.

In relationships, there are many differences between the two individuals. Believe it or not, but opposites do attract. Some of these differences can cause conflict, and some can cause a relationship to grow. In many relationships, there are struggles because we don't always understand why certain differences occur. Most of the time, each wants to feel that they are noticed and have the undivided attention of the other. They also want to feel loved and appreciated. If we feel our partner doesn't notice us, it could lead to us feeling alone. If a woman feels as if she isn't being noticed, most likely she will become depressed, and sometimes this leads to seeking attention from other people. Unfortunately, loneliness can lead to infidelity. Just as we all need to feel noticed, we need to be loved. Some people choose not openly to express their feelings. Many women can be overly emotional when expressing how they feel. For others, they may express their feelings with their actions more than with their words. This may make it difficult for a person to accept someone who expresses themselves differently than what they're used to experiencing. It is at this point that some people fail to be understanding of these differences.

You can't expect the person you are dating to do everything in accordance to your liking. Not only is this unrealistic...it's impossible. Even if you have profound similarities, there are still a few differences. Your life experiences have been different, and this causes different characteristics and prospectives. You should embrace it and respect it as such. Never feel as if doing things their way is the only way and never make them feel the same. Both people should feel comfortable with expressing themselves the way they always have as long as it's not in an offensive manner.

In relationships, there is also the need to have a purpose for each person to be happy. If you are in a relationship where one person dictates everything without allowing the other person to contribute, it could cause that person to feel useless. Neither of you should ever feel as if you don't matter. There should be some things you are in charge of maintaining. When we are stripped of these responsibilities, we can develop feelings of doubt. Ultimately, this could make us seek control in other areas of the relationship. As adults, we need to appreciate what we each 'bring to the table.' We should also be able to co-exist despite our differences.

When it comes to balance in relationships, many times we struggle with compromise. We are all guilty of feeling we are the most giving and believe our companion should have the ability to read our minds. At times, we may feel as though we shouldn't have to tell them what it is needed. Often, the problems that occur in a relationship are due to a lack of communication. When we feel that someone doesn't understand what we are relaying, the inflection of our voices may increase. Raising our tone won't help our significant other better understand. In fact, the issue isn't the lack of being able to hear; it's they didn't comprehend. Yelling or raising your tone out of frustration will never get you the type of reaction you want. This could cause the person to shut down completely. We need to find more suitable methods of communication to fulfill our needs without raising our voices. This is the proper way to minimize any conflict. We can always find a better strategy without forcing someone to become defensive. Truthfully, most people in relationships desire to please each other. The more each feels appreciated, the more initiative will be taken to satisfy each other. Be more supportive and have constructive discussions, so your words won't go in one ear and out the other.

Most importantly, avoid trying to change your significant other. At some point, we have all attempted to change a person we were dating. Your companion should never feel they can't be themselves. You need to accept them the way they are or don't enter into a relationship. The person you're dating isn't a project. Yes, you should want who you're dating to look good at all times, but you shouldn't make them feel as if they're below your standards. This will certainly cause a breakdown in the relationship.

To suggest a person isn't good enough will cause resentment and create an unhappy atmosphere. The person will feel inferior and lose confidence in themselves as well as the relationship. Sometimes, certain comments will come across as more insulting than helpful. We tend to look at the things other people are doing that we deem wrong, without realizing our flaws. Some people won't appreciate you for who you are and can be very self-centered. In many cases, we remain in unhealthy relationships purely for the financial support or other benefits. Either way, the reason is for self-gain and could be the cause of some of your relationship issues. A person will eventually realize they are being used. When that is exposed, the person will leave unless they have low self-esteem or are deeply in love. We should never take advantage of someone for our selfish reasons. There must be an equal contribution to any relationship.

You should also understand the person you're dating and make certain they value what you have to offer. If they don't appreciate you and what you do for them, take it as a sign and move on. Don't make the mistake of staying longer than you should with the hopes of getting married. You should be optimistic, but you need to be realistic as well. Trying to force someone into a lifelong obligation can be tragic. You can turn a person away if they're not ready for the next level of commitment. Do not expect a person to be willing to move forward because you are ready. Have patience and allow it to take its course organically. If it doesn't happen in your current relationship, don't fret because plenty of people are interested in forming a union with the right person.

You need someone that is ready and willing to commit to you. You have to realize that everyone operates differently, and at the rate they feel most comfortable. A person could love you with every fiber of their being, but if they're not ready to take the next step, they won't be fully devoted. This could cause infidelity or push the person into the arms of someone else permanently. So, don't give any ultimatums and keep in mind that timing is everything.

Until there has been an actual commitment, you will be continuously trying to secure a permanent position in their life. Be with a partner who makes you feel like you're winning a prize. Make sure you do your part to ensure your companion feels the same way. You should both feel equally blessed to have each other. No relationship is perfect, but appreciating each other will bring about more happiness. Inspire the person you're dating, so they visualize a brighter future with you as a part of it.

Certain struggles are part of any relationship. But many can be onset if you or your partner display any signs of immaturity. Most people don't like to be confronted about their behavior. You can't correct existing issues if you're unable to accept constructive criticism, without becoming defensive. Sometimes we need to check ourselves to put things in order. If you take a look at your failed relationships with an open mind, you may find areas where you could've dealt with things differently. Most of the time, we repeat the same patterns because we are creatures of habit. We lessen the probability for our next relationship being successful because we don't take the time to work on ourselves. Sometimes we need to 'hit rock bottom,' before we realize we need to make a change. It takes years for us to reach the level of maturity necessary to maintain a healthy relationship.

When we become involved with someone new, we tend to drift away from our friends as we are overwhelmed with anxiety and excitement. We may not have enough free time to juggle our friendship and new relationship. Once you pass that stage, you begin to spend as much time with them as possible. However, it is important not to neglect your friends and family because they have been there much longer than the new person. Of course, you want this relationship to last forever, but there are no guarantees. Chances are, it may not last, so don't shut out the people in your support system. When the 'head over heels' phase passes, our usual routine sets in motion. This is where we may not show each other as much appreciation as we did in the beginning. This can become a problem further down the line, so show them how much they mean to you daily.

Moving a little further in your relationship, you may decide you are ready to take things a step further. Maybe this means moving in together or even getting engaged. Regardless of how this may benefit both of you as a couple, you still need to maintain your financial independence. You should both be independently stable, so if something happens, you can support each other. Financial difficulties can damage a relationship and sometimes beyond repair. Because of this, it should be a priority to keep your finances in order, so you're prepared for the unexpected. As you two move toward becoming one, you have to make some sacrifices, so that things work in your favor. Sometimes, we believe we need to give up on our dreams to keep a person we want. You are a smart, confident and mature woman; you understand that a great relationship should build you up and never tear you down. Having a partner, you love dearly should only bring out the best in you. You should never feel as if you have to give up everything you love to make it work.

Your companion should be willing to stand by you and encourage you to follow all of your dreams; especially if it makes you happy. This is the ideal partner you need. There should never be a battle over which one of you should sacrifice your dreams. This relationship will take work; figure out what's required to keep it together. For each of you, there will be different things that give you satisfaction. It is perfectly normal for each person to have an entirely different idea of what happiness is. You may simply need a personal vanity station to put on your makeup, or he may need his 'man cave,' to enjoy his Sunday football games in peace. You should both be entitled to that. We should never think just because we enjoy something our companion will too. If each person takes the time to let one another know what pleases them, there will be less to work to do in the relationship.

You and your partner are allowed an equal amount of happiness. To eliminate some of the disagreements, both of you should have time to yourselves. Being together all of the time forces you to notice you've both changed from when you first met. This is normal because we change with age and experiences. You should never expect a person to remain the same. While there will be some personality changes, there should never be a change in the level of respect you give each other.

You should never feel it is acceptable to disrespect someone you claim to love unconditionally. You have self-respect and wouldn't allow this type of treatment. The point is; never stop being the person they fell in love with, and always treat each other with the utmost respect.

Don't take each other's feelings for granted. The longer you manage to stay together, the more you should appreciate your companion. You should never have to sacrifice your happiness. Your significant other will do their best to maintain a standard of good living. You won't wonder if they love you or if they care because their actions will show they do. They won't feel the need to be possessive and treat you like property. Your every move won't be checked, and you will be trusted the same way you trust them. They will be very secure with your relationship, and they will be confident that you will be loyal and give your heart and soul.

If you have been blessed to find this person, you should give them just as much as they give you. At this point, you should cherish your relationship. Keep the inner workings of your situation private and keep everyone out of your business. You should avoid discussing the details of your relationship with your friends. Many people who discuss their relationship problems with their friends never realize those same friends never tell them anything about their relationships. Why? Because they know having too many people in your business can lead to problems in the future. So, they are being wise and keeping it to themselves. You should also refrain from discussing any of your relationship problems on social media platforms. You will never get a positive response when spreading your business for everyone give their opinions.

When we decide to make someone our life partner, we still need our personal time to fit into our schedule, no matter how busy we may be. Many of us neglect this personal time, and never realize how much we need it. Life can be very stressful, and once you have the responsibility to make someone else happy, it can become even harder. As you move further into this relationship, there may be times when one of you has more success than the other. 'Such is life.' You will always have one person that excels in their career more than the other. But this should never make you bitter and unable to support them. You should never resent them either because as a couple you share in what your partner achieves. You should be their number one supporter when they take another step in their career. Don't ever be selfish and unsupportive because this could cause irrevocable damage to your relationship.

Another critical thing to remember is that getting into a relationship should never make you lose your identity. You fall in love with a person because of who they are, what they contribute to your life, and how they treat you. Therefore, it is paramount that you remain being 'you.' If you change so much that you become unrecognizable, it could be difficult to sustain the love you have for each other. Never feel as though you have to be what they want you to be and lose your identity in the midst of that. This won't benefit either of you because you'll soon be accused of changing as a person.

It is our hope that this information will help you hone in on what is important when trying to maintain a healthy relationship. There will be bad days and most likely many of them. I would be more concerned with the couple who says they never disagree and have the perfect connection. That isn't a real representation of any relationship. Be honest with yourself and don't feel like you are a failure or that your situation is a disaster because you have an argument from time to time. That is very normal. What isn't normal is constant arguing that never ends with some correcting of issues or resolution. It should also never lead to mental or physical abuse. Having disagreements and being able to talk about them is a sure sign of two mature people with a common goal of being together. If someone feels the need to be demeaning or degrading to you in any way, you should end the relationship as soon as you can. Verbal abuse is a segue to physical abusive in most instances and could impact your next relationship. It is always important to do what makes you happy and is in the best interest of your mental and physical well-being.

The Importance of Education and Using Your Full Potential

Education has always been imperative, but it hasn't always been a requirement. Many men and women in history have been extremely successful without much education. However, it is very rare. In the past years, during the younger years of our grandparents and parents, men were expected to further their education while women were encouraged to marry and bear children. Things have certainly changed during the millennium. Women are now focusing on furthering their education and gaining their independence. We are still very interested in having a family of our own, but we are just as focused on securing our futures. For this reason, you should always work on yourself. You can never have too much education. Educated woman are capable of bringing forth socio-economic change because education is a fundamental right. If you realize the importance of women obtaining a quality education, you can encourage more women to follow your lead. So, what can education do for women? Here are some areas that can be improved with having an education.

1. *Well-educated women are classified with dignity and honor.* Women with education can become an inspiration for young women who look up to them as role models. What better way to use your gifts? It's a rewarding feeling to be a part of another woman's growth. Especially, in a time where our youth are being influenced by television and music that strips away their innocence. We should show them there is another way that doesn't involve the sacrifice of their dignity, morals, and values.

2. *Being well educated can improve your life.* When you are well educated, you have the ability to secure a better paying position providing you with a better

place to live because of your financial stability. A woman with a good education can be more aware of her rights and can demand proper treatment. Being knowledgeable on different subjects also allows you to communicate better and never feel inferior to your male counterparts. With education, a woman's identity as an individual will never be lost.

3. *Education will empower women to become economically independent.* To remain in this position, a woman needs a quality employment and proper education. Education will also empower women to contribute to the development of others. This is important because being selfish will never make a positive change in the future.

4. *Education will give women the ability to choose their profession.* It may not sound like a big deal, but it one of the most significant gains from having an education. One of the greatest feelings is

having a choice in what you do to earn a living. You will never be forced to accept an undesirable occupation because having an education provides you with options. The world opens up to you when you are well educated. You will have an array of opportunities at your fingertips. You should also share this feeling with others and encourage them to strive for equality and greatness.

5. *Being well educated can keep you more informed of your rights for justice.* This could lead to a decline in violence and injustice against women. It can also help eliminate women becoming victims of people with an agenda of exploitation.

6. *Being well educated can help alleviate poverty.* Women who secure better-paying positions can establish some financial stability. We will never be able to eliminate poverty, but a well-educated woman can contribute to making a difference one day at a time.

7. *Education for women can lead to increased literacy.* Studies show that offering education to women could raise literacy rates and push forward development in areas which are struggling.

8. *Education can lead to safe sex and better health.* When women are educated, they are more aware of the risky behavior. Once you know the consequences of not protecting yourself you may be more willing to practice safe sex to protect your health and the health of others as well. As quality education increases, fertility, population growth, and overall health improve.

Education has the power to open your eyes and broaden your horizon. The individual is the first person who will directly benefit from having an education. Then, the effects migrate down to the family because it helps women have a positive influence. There's always someone in your family that everyone admires. The one person that obtained success and has led by example. In your eyes, this person has it all. By using them as an example could lead to greater self-esteem and self-confidence, in which some people may be lacking. This is the contribution to yourself by igniting your potential and inspiring other women to discover their own. Help these young women that you influence work to fully develop themselves and increase their resistance to discrimination. With such a positive impact on their families; areas like health and nutrition would improve. When combined with an improvement in their status, they will play a vital role in improving community and society stability. With more awareness of your position, you can make a difference in helping a struggling environment. Education alone is not the answer to all of the world's problems, but it is an essential factor in developmental advancement.

> *"If you are always trying to be normal, you will never know how amazing you can be."*

> *—Maya Angelou*

There is no secret to reaching your full potential. It takes work, but in the end, it would be well worth it. One issue that arises is when we think we have done our best. For instance, we can progress through grade school and college feeling as if we have given it our all. Often, we are satisfied with being mediocre if it can get us through. It's a travesty to barely get by and accept that we don't need to apply ourselves more. We should always strive to accomplish more, especially when it comes to obtaining an education. Unfortunately, being too complacent is what prevents us from reaching our full potential. If you believe you have arrived at the peak of your potential, then a ceiling has been placed on your ability to expand.

The lack of confidence will most likely prompt you to quit instead of pushing forward. Trust that things won't always be perfect as planned. Regardless of the circumstances, if you believe you can do more; you will. Also, you should live for more than yourself. We were made to be versatile and do more than what works for us. The good is that potential is not finite. Therefore, it could always be adjusted. It's merely a vision that we have to keep us going. We all have the ability to achieve greatness; we just have to gain the necessary knowledge. After you discover you aren't living the life you are meant to live; your full potential will begin calling. No, it isn't an actual voice, but more so a feeling you get when you are ready to display your talents to the world. Here are some of the signs, which should give you that feeling.

- The first feeling you'll experience is anxiety deep down in your stomach. It's a feeling you most likely can't describe with words. This is almost like an alarm clock waking you up. You'll experience intense anticipation similar to a child in a toy store. Your mind will wander all over the place, and a sudden surge of energy will travel throughout your body leaving you with an unsatisfied feeling. Meaning you are finally at a point in your life where you have an uncontrollable need to attain success.

- Another clue is you'll constantly be thinking of ways to change your future. You'll get an influx of ideas, and you'll find it may be difficult to formulate an understanding of these new thoughts. You'll begin to visualize yourself in a better place. Including, financially, physically, mentally, emotionally or spiritually. Whatever the vision, your dreams will start to crystallize into an image of reality.

- We've all read books or stories on the blogs we immediately can relate to our lives. We sit and imagine how different our life would be if we were in their shoes. Sometimes, these stories can make you feel sad about not accomplishing what the other individuals have. It can also do the opposite and inspire you to do more with your life. Sometimes your feelings can confuse you. They can make you happy, angry or sad. The fact that it evokes any emotion is evidence it is time to pursue your full potential.

- Have you ever been in bed and had a hard time falling asleep because your brain is racing? You can hear the voice loud and clear in your ear telling you to get up, get out and do something. The sound continues to nag you regardless of how many times you've tried to shut it up. This is your queue there are great things in your future. When it's time, you'll get the call and your inner self will tell you to work on your plans for the future.

You also have to figure out what you need to do to reach the level you desire. Living to your fullest potential isn't as difficult as you may think. There are many reasons why people fall short of their goal. We've gathered a list of reasons why we fail to reach our full potential.

1. We are all great but still, underestimate ourselves. There is always a voice in our heads saying we aren't good enough and we don't have what it takes to reach our level of greatness. We also make excuses as to why we can't desire a greater degree of success. Often, we justify this way of thinking by being pessimistic because it prepares us for failure. Truthfully, there is no real justification. Sadly, we are very capable of convincing ourselves everything is fine the way it is. There is always a higher level. You should attempt to be more optimistic and realistic about your endeavors.

2. You have to work hard. Another reason we don't reach our full potential is that we can

determine what it is, but be unsure of how we get to the next point. Most people are aware of their potential. We all know what we are capable of when we are at our best. You've most likely had visions about reaching a certain level, which appears to be higher than your current status. Knowing the amount of work you have to do could be very overwhelming. This is no reason to give up or settle for less. Never allow hard work scare you away from greatness.

3. Another reason we don't reach our full potential is that we use too much of our energy focusing on the wrong things. There is no way for you to reach your full potential when you lack the energy and drive needed to do so. If you are sure, your goal involves helping other people focus on that. You can have too many obligations and be unable to apply yourself effectively. If this happens, you'll never be able to handle it all without becoming overwhelmed. There is a possibility this will result in being unproductive regardless of how much time you utilize getting out of the rut. We

weren't meant to live a subpar life. You just have to work very hard to master one component before moving on to the next. Your journey will take you to higher levels sooner than you think. There are some beneficial ways to execute properly, and we've listed them to help you succeed.

- Start by encouraging yourself instead of using pity and self-doubt. No one succeeds at anything in life by beating themselves up for every mistake they've made. You need to be positive and remain motivated. There aren't any perfect people and certainly none who have always made the right choices. The goal is always to do your best and cheer yourself on whenever you can.

- Another option to help during your quest of reaching your full potential is to discover your passions. When you put all, you can muster into something that serves no purpose or fails to make you happy means you're misguided. If something is a passion of yours, it will excite you as well as motivate you. Regardless of how tired you may be, working on this could easily give you the boost of energy you need to move forward. Within these confines is where you can locate your full potential; you just have to realize what it is.

- The next area to help you reach your full potential is by knowing your strengths. The key to reaching your full potential is to understand what you are capable of doing completely. You should be able to list the areas where you are the strongest. Once they are identified, they will be immovable. When you make a list of these strengths, it will be easier to figure out what tools you need to get there. The journey to the top can be a short one. It can also be a long one if you aren't equipped with the things you need to navigate your way through effortlessly.

- Once you have identified your strengths, you can determine your skill gaps. Your power is where you are strong, and you'll be able to identify what areas need additional support. If you are going to improve anything you will need to know what areas need adjusting. It's important to realize both because that will help you navigate through your process much easier. For this to be effective, you have to be brutally honest with yourself. You can't expect to get ahead if you are not transparent.

- The next thing you need to do is decide what you are willing to do so that you can reach your desired goals. Sometimes reaching your full potential requires you to put in very long hours and make some sacrifices that may not be easy. You need to focus on the goal you set for yourself. There will always be time for fun and games later. Besides, you will have much more fun after achieving your goals. You also have to be very committed. There will be some days when you want to give up, but you can't allow yourself to do so. If you realize at any point you can't fully commit; then you are probably at a point where you have divided focus. On this journey, it is fine to take baby steps and work your way to building full focus. You are a body of work in progress, so keep at it and don't give up. However, if you know in your heart this is what you need to do, then, by all means, it is time for you to jump in and get started!

- Now, if you have accepted you aren't fully ready to reach the top, you should figure out the point at which it is too much for you to handle. If you determine this from the onset of your process, you can avoid losing valuable time working on a goal you aren't fully ready to obtain. The sight of succeeding can be blinding at times causing us to become over enthusiastic. This could result in us taking on more than we can handle. Our emotions can spark uncontrollable thoughts, so it may be a good idea to have extracurricular activities in place to give yourself a break, i.e. Yoga.

- It is also critical to have a plan in place when you are on a quest to reach your full potential. Sure, you can attempt to navigate through life without one. However, you could miss a few important steps when you are ill-prepared and take short cuts. The plan doesn't have to be concrete. There is room to make changes along the way. You can create a minimal outline that will categorize your basic goals. You should have some flexibility since you can't foresee the future and any obstacles you may encounter along the way.

- Now that you have established where to go and how to get there: you need to find balance. Many women struggle with finding a balance between work and everyday life. The search for a balanced life can cause more stress than is tolerable. Women typically have a lot to do with their busy schedules. We are mothers, wives, students, business owners and much more. We are expected to stick to our routine even if we are sick, tired or overwhelmed. Women are pleasers, so we often give all of ourselves and not expect reciprocation in any way. We are strong and innately take care of others as well as our homes. Multi-tasking can be a struggle, so take a deep breath and a moment to reflect on your life. This way you can calmly make decisions with a rational mind.

- You also need to focus on energy management. It is very easy to overwork yourself when you work non-stop. Be sure to take the time to eat, drink fluids, exercise and rest. We are all guilty of working non-stop without realizing the amount of damage it is doing to our bodies. You won't be of any value to anyone including yourself if you're admitted to the hospital because you've worked yourself out of commission. In the pursuit of success, we can't neglect one of the most important factors, which is ourselves.

- It is also crucial to make time for motherhood. If you are a mother, it is necessary to spend time in that role. You never want to neglect the chance or take your children for granted. Time doesn't stand still, and you can miss out on milestones in their lives. You'll regret it and never forgive yourself. You'll also regret not giving them the time they needed from you as their caregiver. This is a dilemma for many women, but there is a way to find balance. You have to remain focused, dedicated and you will eventually find a way.

- While you are on a quest to reach your full potential, you may be tempted to make hasty unfavorable decisions. The problem with this is you can run out of steam long before you reach your destination. Having the ability to say 'no' keeps you in control. You should always maintain order because things can quickly become unmanageable.

"Every accomplishment starts with the decision to try."

—John F. Kennedy

There are a few additional areas you should work on to achieve your full potential. This one involves your intuition. By definition, it is the ability to understand something immediately, without the need for constant reasoning. It comes from a combination of experience and instinct. By recognizing what is acceptable by your standards and what is unacceptable can help you make better choices for achieving your potential. You have to trust yourself. If you don't trust yourself, you won't be able to get very far. You know yourself better than anyone else; therefore your intuition can assist you with making better choices. Your intuition is a great tool to utilize during decision-making. Sometimes you need to make decisions very quickly, and in uncomfortable situations, you can do the wrong thing. It is vital during this time to listen and take heed to what your instinct is saying to you. This doesn't mean the decisions will be easier or they'll be the best ones you'll make. However, if you ignore your intuition and make the wrong choice, you'll more than likely come down hard on yourself. By trusting yourself, you'll know you've made the right decision even if you didn't get the desired result.

"You can't have a million-dollar dream with a minimum-wage work ethic."

—Stephen C. Hogan

There is also the subject of business and reaching your full business potential. There is a high possibility this could be even harder to reach than your personal potential. One of the number one factors that hold women back is their lack of confidence. Some women don't believe they can achieve their goals even if they are overqualified. As a woman, we are often at a disadvantage because it is easier for men to move up the corporate ladder. Just because it isn't easy, doesn't mean it is impossible. Even as a woman you should always celebrate your success. Regardless of what the success may be or how unimportant you may think it is; it should be celebrated. A woman should always be brave in business. If you let them see you're nervous or unsure of yourself, you will fall victim to your insecurities. We all have fears, especially in business. We often have people admiring our success so that may be pressure sometimes. This is where we should face these concerns head-on so that we can overcome them. You should also never undermine yourself because there is a line of people who will enjoy watching you fail. Don't give them the satisfaction. It is always important to believe in yourself and all that you are. You must know there is always something inside of you that is greater than any obstacle you may face. Great leaders don't set out to be leaders.

Instead, they set out only to make a difference. Being positive in a negative situation is also needed. Be sure to do it with passion, and you won't fail as long as you don't give up. The key is to hold on to the vision and always trust the process.

There are some questions you can ask yourself. You need to establish what you want others to think of you. If you want to succeed in business, you have to represent yourself to the world in the best way possible. This includes your health, the way you carry yourself and the way you treat others. You don't have to eliminate fun, but you should always be serious regarding your appearance. Some will think they can take advantage of you, so you should always appear focused and driven. While you are on your way to the top, you should have a point of view. You should stand for something publicly and make sure you remain consistent. There will be people who are watching and ready to pull you apart. You must take chances and network. Placing yourself in professional circles is important. You'll be surprised how much you can learn during a business conversation. You should find people who are in your field and learn from them.

Having ambition is vital to making it to the

next level. Without ambition, you'll most likely remain in the same place and never experience any growth. Your purpose is still reaching your full potential, so you should always be driven and passionate about your goals. Without ambition, it is also easy to be overlooked. Keep your eye on the prize and learn the skills you need to acquire what you want to achieve. If you are passionate, no one will be able to change your mind or doubt your capabilities. During a time where it is easy to have self-doubt, having a mentor could help you build your confidence. Having someone in your field will be able to guide you and possibly empathize with the daily stress you may experience. You should be prepared for adversity because it is inevitable. Everyone at some point gets knocked down, but this doesn't mean you aren't worthy or trying hard enough. This is where your resilience needs to be reinforced. When you are off your path, your strength comes from your ability to force your way back. After a fall, you have to give yourself time to recover. You'll have to pick up the pieces and restart the process. Ideally, because now you can set some more goals. Just make certain they're realistic, manageable and attainable. Once the shock has worn off, you'll be able to reconnect and work your way to the top. In addition to these situations, you should prepare yourself for confrontation. In business, women will most likely try to avoid confrontation, but sometimes you can't avoid it, so you'll need to diffuse the situation as best you can.

In business, there will always be work, and us women should stick together. We should also work on inspiring other women in business. Some women have the tendency to appear jealous because we don't always congratulate each other when we accomplish greatness. If you can reach your full potential in your personal life, your business life or both, you will inspire others whether you planned to or not. They may admire you in silence, but inside they want to know what you did to reach that level. We often look at successful celebrities for inspiration, but there are many women in arms reach that are very successful; we just fail to notice. Most women want to be a part of something great. They want to use their gifts, and they would love to shine, but they lack the drive needed to get there.

The challenge is that it's not easy to be inspired on a constant basis. It's very easy to get distracted when we aren't fulfilled. When things don't move quickly enough, we grow impatient. Sometimes this could be fixed by focusing. Dig deep and remember all of the things you did to get as far as you are. You don't want to fall back into your comfort zone and get stuck there. Complacency can destroy you if you let it. You should avoid this at all costs because you've worked too hard to go backward. You won't reach your destination once you are comfortable with where you are in your life. Stay motivated by patting yourself on the back each time you move forward. There are always people who have the same goals as you, especially in business. The moment you lose focus and take your foot off the gas, that individual who has been waiting in the wings will swoop in and take your place. There is nothing worse than working so hard and then allowing someone to take your spot.

You have to develop an unstoppable drive. If your goal is to surpass what you feel is your full potential, you must maintain your drive. You have to want to achieve your goals more than anything else in the world and be prepared to do whatever it takes. Have you ever heard that failure is the prerequisite to success? It is true that failure could lead to success but the only time this would happen is when you are persistent and determined.

Otherwise, that failure will leave you right where you are watching other people reach the level where you want to be.

"Business that makes nothing but money is a poor business."

—Henry Ford

Motivation is a powerful tool. You can move mountains when you are motivated to do so. While you work your way to the top, don't be afraid to grab someone's hand and take them with you. Just as you expect someone to help you on your way, so does everyone else. Even if this makes you a little uncomfortable, you will be rewarded for it. Follow your heart because you know that it is genuine. The reality is that you may be helping someone get ahead who may never pay it forward, but that isn't your issue. When you do something from the heart, you do it without needing something in return. You are on your way to the top, and you will reach the top as long as you follow these tips.

Your full potential is in arms reach, but you have to want it so badly you can't sleep. You can't think of anything else more important to you. There is something to be said about a successful woman that had a dream and put in all of the work needed to get there. If you take a look at many of the great figures throughout history, you'll learn they experienced adversity on more than one occasion. You will also learn they did things they had never done before. Just because something hadn't happened before, certainly doesn't mean it can't be done. The one thing most people lack is they don't carry all of the things one needs to make it happen. You have to be willing to fail and be prepared to fight harder than you thought was physically possible if that means you will succeed. The road to success is always long and hard. Things will get much easier the longer you stick with it.

Whatever your mission is you should know with great power comes great responsibility. That is what separates the greats from everyone else in the world. You have to remember the prize is never about what you win; it's about who you've become in the process. This reward is something you have to earn even though it belongs to you and could never be taken away. Don't ever bury your mistakes and don't fail to take responsibility for your actions. Remember that you are human. You will get tired, you will get stressed, you will get overwhelmed and you will want to give up. You should be productive and never procrastinate. You have to continue to keep your productivity at a high level and stay victorious as you work your way to the top. Always surround yourself with positive people because they have the ability to support you along your journey. Do something today you will thank yourself for in the future. When you know you are destined for greatness, you won't feel complete until you succeed. Your success is waiting for you ahead...claim it.

"If you haven't found it yet, keep looking."

—Steve Jobs

Style, Class, and Substance

When I think of women with style and substance, I think of First Ladies like Jackie Kennedy and Michelle Obama. When I think of grace, I see a woman with confidence and class. A woman should be able to walk into a room and be the center of attention without the need to show their physical assets. Women should have the ability to be stylish without carrying themselves in a way that makes people question their integrity. Women who carry themselves this way are often considered very superficial. When a woman has class, she is deemed exceptional. Sometimes men are afraid to approach a lady of a certain caliber because they assume they won't meet her standards. Most women with substance don't typically have the entitled attitude. They are often the nicest people you'll ever meet. They are very kind, respectful to everyone and always appropriate in a public setting.

These are the women most men dream of dating, but may never meet. As women, we should always carry ourselves in a classy manner and watch with whom we associate. You could be the classiest woman in the world, but if you hang with a group of women with different values, people will assume you are just like them. If you are a mature woman with substance, you wouldn't be comfortable socializing with people who could diminish your reputation. You will likely never find a woman of class fraternizing with individuals who are being disrespectful. She is not your average 'around the way girl.' If you want to be classy, first you will have to change your mindset. A classy woman knows her worth. She walks, talks and acts appropriately. It's not designer clothes that make her who she is; class exudes from her pores. One conversation with her, and you can see the amount of substance she possesses. We want to encourage other women and show them there is a right and wrong way of doing things to succeed in life. If you do not act like you are someone important, then no one else will believe you are.

"For beautiful eyes, look for the good in others; speak only words of kindness; and for poise, walk with the knowledge that you are never alone."

—Audrey Hepburn

A woman with style, class, and substance is a woman of high value. She values the feelings of others, and she is very considerate of their feelings. You must be true to who you are and always be the same person. You can't be classy today, trashy tomorrow and expect people to respect you the same. How can you demand respect if you don't respect yourself? To be perceived as a woman of prestige you have to give them that vision consistently. They will never assume you are a woman of high value if you present yourself without dignity and pride. Stereotypically, when people think of a woman without class, they picture someone without drive or purpose. She only lives for the moment and doesn't have any set standards. Her priorities are not in order because she is not concerned with being responsible. The thought of paying her bills on time is non-existent because she spends her money frivolously not caring about the affect it has on her credit. She's more concerned with having name brand items than having money in her bank account.

Some women are very concerned with impressing people by flaunting their material things. These are the women that will be sure to position their feet in the photo so that you can see the red color of the sole. This is the woman that makes you cringe when she walks into the room. She is the woman that thinks she shows her strength by yelling and over talking you to prevent you from getting a word in edgewise. She's too self-absorbed to care about what you have to say anyway. When a woman values herself, she will never lower her standards by being in the company of the type of women just described.

When it comes to the way that you portray yourself, it starts from within. You have to know what your worth is and what you need to do to receive the proper treatment. You have to work hard to accomplish your goals. A woman with substance would never settle for anything less. Although she has to work as the manager, her goal is to become the CEO one day. Her thought is to be grateful for having her current position while working towards securing a higher one. Why not work your way up the ladder of success? A good way to set goals and encourage yourself to achieve them is to design yourself a vision board. To some people, this may seem like a waste of time. Especially someone that has no interest in pursuing a better career. A vision board can be very useful because you can have a daily reminder of where you want to go in life. The board should be full of things that inspire you and keep you focused.

Inspirational quotes are also excellent to have but make sure they are quotes that mean something to you. You shouldn't just write down a bunch of random quotes from the internet because they sound good. The words are supposed to make you feel inspired and connected with the meaning of the quote. The words should be more relatable than likable. This vision board should bring your images in your mind to life. You should begin with your goals and aspirations. You could have one main goal, or you can have many. You could take a bunch of magazine clippings or print things from the internet to use in your decorating. You want to be sure that while you are creating your vision board, it should be fun. Don't turn it into a job or you won't enjoy it. You could end up creating a vision board that doesn't inspire you to do anything at all. That would totally defeat the purpose. As you work on your vision board, you should pay close attention to how you feel. When you look at a specific photo, it should evoke some emotion. If you look at a picture and it reminds you of a time when you weren't as happy, that should also be used for your vision board. There is nothing more inspiring than seeing where you began. There is no perfect life, and we will all experience storms on our way to the sunlight. You'll be surprised how good you will feel to see your dreams every day. It will make you realize how the things that you aspire to achieve are within arm's reach.

"If I have to, I can do anything. I am strong, I am invincible, I am woman."

—Helen Reddy

There are some things you should introduce into your life to ensure you become the classy woman you strive to be. You could develop some things that could keep you focused, such as meditation or Yoga. Another tip is listening to a particular playlist that is full of music that can give you the push you need. It will never be easy to do anything that is considered great. It will take time and patience, and you will have to keep yourself going when you feel like giving up. Whenever you have moments of self-doubt, you need to encourage yourself. A woman that knows her worth will understand there will be days where a self-talk is needed because positive reinforcement is necessary.

You should also be there to help another woman that may be on the same quest. You'll feel even better about yourself when you make it to the finish line and look to your right to see your sister standing next to you. A woman with class believes this with conviction. She doesn't look at herself as a failure, and she doesn't look at another woman that she's helped as one either. She isn't a fixer-upper, she is just another woman with a dream. Too often we see women tear each other down. They see a woman that has herself together and will still look for flaws. I mean she could be drop-dead gorgeous, smart, talented and finically stable, but somehow they will find something to talk about negatively. It could be something as petty as pointing out the fact that her eyebrows aren't the same length. Sometimes people can be treacherous when envy enters their hearts. If you are a woman with class, you will also know how to keep your composure.

Sometimes people can be very mean and say hurtful things when they are upset. It is important for a woman to think before she speaks because words can be as sharp as swords. There will be times where it will be tough to remain calm, but a woman should never have to raise her voice to get her point across. She is great with words and knows how to be calm and 'sting with her bite, not her bark.' You should have the mindset that allows you to ignore the nonsense. Move forward and know it isn't necessary to cause damage for you to feel better or more important. You can't erase any embarrassment you may have caused by acting like a fool in public. It is much better to walk away from a situation. This will show how confident you are in yourself. It is far from easy, and we all have had moments where we have stepped a little out of character. The only person that you can control is yourself, so you should never give into the negativity. You will be so much more valued and respected this way.

"If you are always trying to be normal, you will never know how amazing you can be."

—*Maya Angelou*

Both men and women notice our posture. I'm sure you've been told that standing tall with your head held high shows confidence. You can't expect anyone to respect you if you're walking around with your head down low, and your shoulders slumped over. You would never believe how much your posture says about you. People are typically more attracted to others that have great posture because it displays a sense of confidence. It is one of the best ways to market yourself, and you'll feel better about who you are at the same time. You have to be conscious of your body language. You may think people don't pick up on it, but they do.

Being a woman doesn't mean you have perfect self-control. What it does say that you have is resilience. You have the capacity to recover quickly from difficult and unfortunate situations. This is a gift not many people have because it's a blessing to be able to withstand the pressures of adversity. It takes a strong woman to go through some extreme lows, but still be able to walk into a building with her head held high. Her confidence is high, and most want to be like her. She is transparent and authentic at all times. When you are a woman of substance, you are never fake. You won't act as if you are happy because 'acting' isn't real. You will be happy, and you will make sure that you wear it all across your face. You aren't into any false advertising because everything about you is real. You should never let your stress show on your face. Even if you've just experienced the worst heartbreak ever, you should remain in control of your emotions.

Class has absolutely nothing to do with emotions. You have to be able to maintain your composure and be able to express your feelings in the appropriate place and the appropriate way. When you are in the comfort of your home, by all means, you could fall out on the floor, cry, scream or yell, but in public, you should remain poised and composed. You should acknowledge the pain. It is normal for you to have feelings and to express them. If you have one person that you trust and you can confide in you should spend some time venting and talking through your frustrations. To truly be authentic you have to value being real more than being anything else. If you struggle with your identity or you're confused about who you should be, it could become a serious issue. At some point, it could totally consume you. You cannot be what other people want you to be. Sometimes, women are looked down upon when they express their feelings in a natural way. Because of this, we feel as though we need to mask our real emotions. We also believe people will view us as weak. This can be the root of an identity struggle between being yourself or being what people want you to be. You shouldn't become stressed and so emotional that you take away from your authenticity. It is always better to be the real you at all times. You have to remain true to yourself to progress on any level. Stay faithful to all of the things that make you who you are. Invest time into your appearance to make sure you are the person you desire to be. You should also exude femininity and have the look of a very well put together person. Sometimes women get into relationships and begin to let themselves go. They get very comfortable and slowly their appearance changes into a person that looks entirely different. To continuously present yourself with an unpleasant look shows you aren't feeling great about who you are and how you look. If you are confident, you would never let your appearance fall by the wayside. You cannot be a successful woman if you don't care about the way you look.

"You are enough, without anyone else's stamp, without anyone else's validation or approval."

—Brandi Harvey

As a classy woman, you should never flaunt your advantages. You don't have to brag and boast to appear relevant. When you are doing well for yourself, it shows, and there will be no doubt about it. No one needs to know your credit score or your net worth. They shouldn't know about the material items you own or about the amount of money you spend. Being able to flaunt what others don't, won't make you, but can surely break you. A woman of class understands that idolizing superficial things are a distraction from more important issues in the real world. The hidden qualities that you have will put a glow around you wherever you may be. A classy woman knows that everyone deserves respect. Certain situations will require a different response, but that response should not equate to disrespect. Always respect your parents and your elders. As a classy woman, you will know the importance of addressing people with their appropriate titles.

A characteristic of a classy woman is her innate ability to assist others when she can. If she sees a homeless person in need, she'll have no problem placing money in their cup to buy food. She knows that falling on hard times could happen to anyone, including herself. Sometimes we see a person on the corner asking for help, and if their clothes aren't tattered, we think they probably aren't really in need of aid. The reality of this is that you don't need to be out panhandling to be struggling. Many people have a place to live, but their bills may be severely past due. They could have lost their job or suddenly become ill. A change in income could cause things to spiral out of control quickly. We have all had a situation where we may have lived paycheck to paycheck. So what gives us the right to look down upon them? Sometimes, people just need a little bit of help. If you decide to give, do it from the heart and do not expect anything in return. If they take the money and use it for anything other than food, it's out of your control.

A woman with class and substance is friendly. Not because she is fake, but because she is a genuine person. She has a great heart and sees the best in people. She walks with a smile on her face because she truly is happy. She understands there is nothing wrong with greeting strangers or replying to a stranger with a simple 'hello.' To be a pleasant person does not mean you have to engage in a conversation. However, she isn't uncomfortable when someone she doesn't know sparks a general discussion. It's not a crime to be kind.

"A rose can never be a sunflower, and a sunflower can never be a rose. All flowers are beautiful in their own way, and that's like women too."

—Miranda Kerr

To be classy, you must also focus on your attitude and self-improvement. There are always some areas that you can improve. Never get to a point in your life where you feel you are too perfect to make any changes. When it comes to a woman of substance, she will never objectify herself. She is someone whose life has meaning and purpose. Her life is filled with love as well as passion. Just like a lady with class, she isn't materialistic as those things don't define her. She will allow her clothing only to accentuate the gifts she already has.

When you are a woman of substance, things are done the way you want, but not with offensive intent. She never feels the need to apologize for who she is because she is who she was meant to be. What other people think is not her concern because she makes her decisions and owns them. She controls her life and everything in it. Her driven mindset is untouchable and fuels her ambition. She is very aware of her worth and doesn't have time to waste on anything unproductive. Her time is valuable, so she would never waste anyone else's time. She always searches for ways of making herself better and focusing on her happiness. If one doesn't value her time, she doesn't hesitate to push them out of her life. She will never sit and sulk when things don't go her way.

Life is about grabbing it by the horns and keep pushing through. There isn't room for impatience and self-doubt. She is confident and has belief in her capabilities. This woman may not know everything about life but anticipates the curveballs coming her way. She is a woman that falls but gets back up each time. She would never spend time around people who judge her. Other's opinions are expected, but trying to demean her is unacceptable. She is accountable for her mistakes and thankful for them because every experience in life is a blessing or a lesson. The mistakes she makes can be turned into something great. She will encourage other women to do the same. Innately, she is a protector, so she would never tolerate inappropriate treatment of others. She is always a realist, and will always be honest even when it could hurt someone's feelings. She knows how important it is to be truthful, so she doesn't do it maliciously. She is a woman that loves to laugh. She knows there is a time to be serious, and knows you shouldn't be serious all of the time.

"A girl knows her limits, but a wise girl knows she has none!"

—Marilyn Monroe

A woman of substance is a woman of meaning and power. It is a badge of honor to be branded as such. It is one of the greatest compliments that you could give to a woman. She has character as well as morals and principles. Her personality is something special and is infectious to others around her. She is a woman that is admired by many because she represents what they aspire to be. A woman of substance is very humble as she has dignity. She has unyielding values and is someone everyone is interested in getting to know. When she finds her purpose in life, she will be sure to work on the things she needs to fulfill it. She is a woman willing to do whatever it takes to make her dreams a reality. A woman of substance has a plan a, b and c as a contingency for when things don't go as planned. She knows it is important to think of different scenarios and outcomes. She will always hope for the best, but she will also prepare for the worst. A woman of substance will never give up regardless of how tough things get. She is a go-getter, and she will never surrender the things she has worked so hard to achieve. She also knows when a situation is not healthy and will make the decision to walk away before she ever allows her safety to be in jeopardy. A woman of substance will always stand up for what she believes in. When asked her opinion, she will say what she thinks, but knows when it's time to speak and when it isn't. She is the one that other people come to for advice because she is often the voice of reason and intelligence. She is a woman that will always stand on her own two feet without the need to lean on anyone else.

> *"She's been through hell and came out, an angel. You didn't break her, darling. You don't own that kind of power."*

> *—BMM Poetry*

She will never sit around and wait for someone to make things happen for her. A woman of substance must stand for what she believes in. She motivates and inspires the women in her circle. A woman of substance is more assertive and persuasive, in fact, she is always willing to take a risk when no one else will. A woman of substance will always follow her heart but doesn't have random one night stands. She will get to know the person to begin a relationship with a solid foundation. To her, it is important to build a lasting relationship and not shuffle people in and out of her life. She values her body and her health. So, she is a woman who cherishes her body like a temple, and would rather save herself for her future significant other. A woman of substance knows that if she wants to have a great relationship she has to make it happen. She knows that a relationship will take work, so she is willing to do what is needed to be with the person she wants.

A woman of substance would never feel the need to compete with another woman because she doesn't view her as competition. She knows how important it is to empower each other instead of tearing down one another. She understands the meaning of sisterhood and how women should look out for each other. Other women's success inspires her to raise the bar on her goals. She knows that having a negative mindstate does not lead to a positive life. A woman of substance knows that if you think happy thoughts it will make a significant change in your life. She knows that focusing on other people more than you focus on yourself, hinders your progression. A woman of substance has no problem supporting another woman in her endeavors. She knows that a little bit goes a long way. One of her greatest attributes is believing that people helping each other make the world a better place. A woman of substance will embrace natural beauty and natural hair. If she wears makeup and hair extensions, she will never degrade another woman for her choice to wear neither one. A woman of substance knows she could influence others. She is a QUEEN! She will uplift other women and let them know they are QUEENS too! A woman of substance knows when strong women unite and focus on a goal, together they can make a difference in the world. She knows it's important to lend a shoulder when another woman needs it. Also, she wouldn't go out and tell someone's business that was shared with her in confidence. A woman of substance finds great value in her friends. She knows how important it is to maintain genuine friendships. She admires other women's strength, and she will be there in times of need. Her passion for helping other women become stronger runs deep because she too has been broken and has had failures.

"Elegance is when the inside is as beautiful and the outside."

—Coco Chanel

A woman of substance is never insecure and doesn't have a problem sharing her knowledge. She realizes that life is already complicated enough, so her true fulfillment comes from passing it forward. She knows that when she helps one person, it helps other people as well. If more people took queues from her, they would see how much of a blessing it is to share knowledge with others. She believes having happiness brings forth a more productive life. Being selfless is a rare character trait. A woman of substance knows if other people see her values and giving nature it could transform their life. If possible, she will share more than knowledge. She knows you can't expect to receive blessings with a closed hand. You have to open your hands to gain whatever is being given to you. She is proud to be a woman and knows the importance of strengthening others. She is intentional with her giving and is willing to give her all to those that deserve it.

We make decisions daily that could have major effects on our lives. We have to ensure that we follow our hearts and do what we feel is right. There will always be distractions and obstacles in our way to prevent us from reaching our goals. When you watch Michelle Obama walk onto a stage, you see a beautiful woman with confidence. You see a woman that speaks eloquently and radiates intelligence. She grabs your attention in any situation because she is the perfect combination of style, grace, and relatability. When you see her attire, it always expresses her individuality from head to toe. Everything is professional and appropriate. You should never expect anything less from a woman comfortable within herself. When you meet a woman with class, she will make a statement without saying a word. You'll see her shine and view her as the definition of amazing. She is the woman that gives from the heart without hesitation, will help someone in need, inspires other woman and knows the real value of 'sisterhood.' She has goals and knows they are within her reach. She is a woman that will never allow anyone else to define her because she will be everything she wants to be. She is an asset and should be appreciated. This type of woman handles herself with respect. She loves herself, and she will never make any excuses. She is thankful for the life she has been given but is confident enough to work towards a better one. If you are blessed enough to befriend this woman, be thankful, grateful and grab your journal to take notes; for a woman with style, class, and substance is inside of all of us.

Holding Grudges, Coping with Insecurities and Anger

There are certain things men just don't understand about women and our emotions. As women, our moods often fluctuate. We can blame it on a number of things, including our hormones. Then, there is that time of the month when sometimes everyone needs to stay out of our way. There are days we don't even understand our mood swings; laughing one minute and crying hysterically the next. Of course, there are many things about men we don't understand either. We are programmed very differently, so there will always be confusion when it involves the unknown.

At times, we can find the smallest thing to upset us. It can be a minuscule issue, but sometimes we overreact as if it was something detrimental to our health and welfare. Other times, we may be inclined to hold a grudge because, under certain circumstances, an apology doesn't suffice. We have to be ready to forgive and get over situations. We are headstrong and sometimes won't accept being told what to do. It's at our discretion that we determine why we should let things go. We believe we are entitled to our feelings and it's pointless to attempt to deny a woman that right.

Sure, some women have the tendency to be irrational, and some of us may be the best at controlling our anger. Some would say there is a double standard as if men don't have the tendency to behave the same in certain situations. Most likely, both males and females would agree that the other holds grudges longer. Regardless of your sex, as an adult, you should be able to resolve conflict without getting out of control or feeling as though things need to escalate to a physical confrontation. This type of behavior is unacceptable and shows a lack of maturity. Typically, people with anger issues aren't the easiest to converse with or confront about their problems with conflict resolution. They'll most likely feel attacked and feel the need to be defensive.

There isn't a simple way to discuss anger, and it could become a very uncomfortable situation for everyone. Often, this could make things far worse before they get any better. This is a real issue, and unless we learn the proper way to resolve conflict, we won't have any lasting relationships. People tend to be very hurtful in the heat of an argument, and 'words can cut deep.' Some anger leads to destructive patterns that could do damage. Many people have experienced pain they were unable to shed. They've been angry about something that may have happened years ago or even in their childhood. You could never put a timeframe on someone's feelings towards a situation that has impacted their life. Just because you have been able to move past some cases doesn't mean the next person will. Getting over hurt takes time and being able to forgive someone is more complicated than people think. Hell, most individuals who say they've been able to get over something most times haven't. They'd rather bury it and pretend as if it never happened, then, later on, that same issue resurfaces. Unless you have truly dealt with the pain, the anger will never go away; it's in hibernation until the next time someone evokes that emotion. I've been there many times before and sometimes you have to hit rock bottom before you realize you need to make a change to balance your psyche. It is time to learn how to effectively communicate about something that has hurt you physically or emotionally.

People have their theories when it relates to the way women deal with their anger. As we mentioned before, unless you address the triggers they will never be corrected. Many personality traits can explain these behaviors. Women sometimes have high emotions that can come across off as unreasonable. Because some of us aren't aware of our conduct, we believe our actions are acceptable and thus conclude we aren't emotional. During this time, no one can convince us to think otherwise. Some of us find ourselves in hostile situations, where we may even have to engage in physical altercations, without taking responsibility for our part in the drama. We could go on for days and weeks and still refuse to take any accountability. In a perfect world, our actions would always be justified, but that's not reality. Realistically, at some juncture, we have all been in the wrong. As we look back to that time, we wish we would have dealt with the situation much differently. For this reason, it is vital to think about your actions and outcome before you act inappropriately. Once you execute your actions, you can't reverse them. An apology may not always repair the situation. Besides, repetitive behavior validates a person's true intent, concluding that an apology would be baseless.

When speaking about anger, we all have had our fair share of angry moments. Although, some cases may have been more severe than others. Nevertheless, the difference is one group of individuals may be able to regain their composure while others quickly spiral out of control without the use of any restraint. Many women lack this ability. Maybe they were raised in a home where arguing and fighting often occurred. It's possible the endless arguments eventually turned into physical fights. To most people, this is dysfunctional, and they would never allow themselves to live in an environment with such turmoil. For others, they may have experienced this during their childhood, so they were forced to live in this environment. Unfortunately, they were too young to leave, so this is all they know. When you live in this type of atmosphere, you respond to this one of two ways: you believe this is normal or you run at first sight of anything like it. You could continue through life always in and out of these emotional states. Eventually, you begin to think this is the way it should be. This becomes your normality, and any confrontation anyone has with you are believed to be their fault. A person who justifies their actions is convinced whoever disagrees deserves whatever actions are displayed towards them. This is a clear indication this individual doesn't have control over their emotions.

Women often use their emotions to guide them in everyday life. Sometimes, we use our feelings more than our brains. You should never get comfortable with being irrational. If you're unable to look within yourself and realize you may have a problem, there's a possibility you will remain in a never-ending cycle of emotional stress. Amongst other issues, anger in some women could be a result of these emotions; similar to a chronic disease. However, this can be remedied if you work to change the way you act. Some women use anger as a defense mechanism. We feel as though we have to portray this abrasive image to protect ourselves and ward off people from confronting us. Sometimes this may stem from insecurities or habits we've had for years.

There are plenty of women that aren't exhibiting this type of behavior. In relationships, there are far more who act this way and don't realize it. If we find that we are uncomfortable or don't trust our significant other like we should, this can lead us to stress. The stress then sparks the irrational display of anger. When we view things as threats, we lose our sense of security. Even if we have ourselves together or have someone that loves us unconditionally; many of us are insecure about certain aspects of our lives. We may never admit it to anyone or even to ourselves.

Some relationships have separated over the notion, but not the actual violation. The constant arguing caused the relationship to become tumultuous resulting in the sudden breakup. Many of us have experienced a fear that our companion isn't committed to our relationship. This could be because you're aware of things that have happened in their previous relationship. Maybe they admitted they had been unfaithful on a few occasions in the past. We automatically assume we'll experience that same fate. You know the saying, "Once a cheater always a cheater," and this constantly replays in our minds. We can't automatically conclude the same thing will be done to us. Besides, if you feel this way, you should consider restoring your trust. If not, it's probably best to not continue the relationship.

To have a healthy and productive relationship, we can't make the person feel uncomfortable. No one wants to feel as though they have to reassure their companion they're faithful constantly. Even after all of the reassurances, we may still have some insecurities. If we continuously doubt the person we're dating, they could become incredibly conflicted and confused. They'll wonder if this relationship is worth all of the trouble. Somehow, we will still find a reason to blame them for our self-imposed trust issues. The last thing a person wants is to be accused of are false allegations and their honesty put in question. This heightened level of emotion and insecurity will start a chain of events that could lead to disaster. We have to learn how to communicate our feelings without the involvement of anger. Especially, if we want to be in a committed relationship with someone we love. This behavior supports an imbalance of confidence in the person you're dating and could push them away instead of pulling them closer to you.

At least once in our lives, we've all most likely had stronger feelings for someone that didn't reciprocate the same to us. This could turn into a very awkward situation when we learn we aren't on the same page with each other. In a moment like this, some of us may feel the desperation to be noticed by them or go above and beyond our normal actions to gain their affection. This could make us appear extremely clingy. We'll always be more concerned about losing the person than we are about keeping them. This could result in the opposite reaction than the one you're trying to obtain from the individual. If things don't go our way, even the strongest woman could feel as if she's inadequate and may feel incapable.

It's possible to feel disdain when we have been rejected or misunderstood. At some point, we need to reflect and identify what may be causing the issues. You can't move from relationship to relationship without addressing them. If the aforementioned is typical in the way you act at times, then you have to allow time to take its course when you begin to change. However, because your actions may be habitual doesn't make them acceptable. Anger is a natural emotion that may be triggered and expressed, so displaying the emotion is only part of the issue. The other part is being honest with ourselves and accepting that we should exhibit better behavior.

If we attempt to cover up all of our feelings by putting on makeup and glamming up ourselves, will not address the internal issues. The only thing can change that is the realization that you have an issue. You have to want things to be better for you. Just because it's comfortable being a certain way doesn't mean that it's the way that your life was supposed to be. There are a few healthy ways to express anger: vent to a friend, scream into your pillow or in your car, write down your feelings on paper and speak to the person you're angry with in a healthy way. Healthy anger is a very powerful tool that is functional. Anger becomes dysfunctional when it works against our best interest. Anger is an instinctive reaction. It is anger which has been redirected from its source into socially acceptable forms of expression, which comes in many forms. These types refer to dysfunctional patterns in the way that we display this emotion. If we aren't able to work on our anger by ourselves, it would be beneficial to find out how to get professional assistance for anger management.

There are many other ways of expressing and managing anger. All of these may be detrimental and should be corrected. One of the forms of expression is resentment, which is the constant replaying of a feeling, and the events leading up to it, that goads or angers us. This can lead to blaming and deep-seated hostility. Chronic resentment creates a passageway for passive-aggressive behavior and acting out inappropriately. This is a form of unhealthy anger which could consume us as well as cause damage to our mental health. Expression of another kind is aggression, which is the overt, often harmful, social interaction with the intention of inflicting damage or other unpleasantness upon another individual. It is destructive and often very hurtful. Behaviors that can be associated with anger include domestic violence, fist fights, road rage and aggressive driving. These behaviors can have very devastating consequences. There are many people in prison today for allowing their aggression to put them in an irreversible situation. There is also verbal abuse, which is one of the most common forms of unhealthy anger. Verbal abuse, which is described as a negative defining statement told the victim or about the victim, or by withholding any response, thereby defining the target as non-existent. This is also a form of verbal bullying that can often do psychological damage to the victim.

Then, there is what is termed as repressed anger, which is a feeling of tension and hostility that one holds inside until an eruption, usually caused by anxiety aroused by a perceived threat to one's self, possessions, rights, or values. This emotion is avoidable if issues with others are addressed sooner. It can lead to depression which could cause individuals to harm themselves. In many cases, it can be undetectable until it's too late.

The display of passive-aggressive anger, which can take many forms but can generally be described as a non-verbal aggression that manifests in negative behavior. This is the instance where you are angry with someone but do not or cannot tell them. However, this type of aggression rarely goes unnoticed. Unfortunately, there are many people with judgmental anger, which is caused by unfavorable judgments made about other individuals or situations and is again a form of resentment or loathing. Some people see the need to throw rocks while living in a glass house. You know those that have something negative to say about everyone as if they have the perfect fairytale life. This form of anger causes people to criticize other individuals with the intention of making themselves feel better about their shortcomings.

The criticism can be extremely harsh and malicious. With obsessive anger, which emits the feelings of jealousy and envy, one could easily destroy someone's self-worth and security. This could lead to angry outbursts and other forms of anger that may be out of your control.

There are also those that experience rage, which is violent, uncontrollable anger. It's not common for most people, but there are many cases where a person killed someone and didn't remember what caused their actions. This could stem from years of suppressed anger which could be unrelated to the situation where the explosion occurs. When it pertains to rage, some extremes need to be corrected before 'traveling down the path of no return.' While some forms of anger are a physiological disorder, which brings about these outbursts they can only be treated with medication.

Sure some men suffer from these various types of anger issues, so this isn't only an issue for women. In life, we will all be hurt, and we will most definitely all be upset, but we have to find it within ourselves to forgive. When you hold grudges, you are giving someone else the power that you should hold. You should never allow that to happen. Instead of focusing on something positive you find yourself wasting a lot of time being miserable. There are certain things about forgiveness that we have to keep in mind, and the first involves apologies. For some reason, we tend to think that the only way that we can forgive someone for doing something wrong is for them to apologize verbally. Accepting an apology doesn't constitute that the person has to remain in your life. Once someone does you wrong, you could lose trust in them which is very hard to regain. Ergo, no one can tell you that you need to keep the person in your life. You have the right to forgive and still remove them from your circle. When you forgive someone, it doesn't mean that you forgot what they've done to you. The memory will always remain a part of your life. You are allowed to have the memory without living the situation over and over.

Forgiveness can be challenging when you were violated by someone that you love. I believe that if you truly love someone, you wouldn't intentionally hurt them. Everyone makes mistakes, but committing the same offense is no longer a mistake; it is a choice. So if you've done something to hurt someone once, and then do it again, that means you don't care about their feelings.

As women, it is important to work on the issues that will make you a better version of yourself. Allowing any of these things to control you is a hindrance to your success. When you have a purpose, you have to live in it, and you need to cut ties with anything that could prevent you from achieving your goals. If you are at a point in your life where you have tried everything possible, and you still can't find a way to move on, reach out for some professional help. You should never be embarrassed about seeking additional assistance. Maybe one day you'll be able to help another person in the same situation.

You can use your knowledge and past experiences to be a mentor. Show the individual that there is a better way and a light at the end of the tunnel. It's hard when "You can't see the forest for the trees," but believe us the moment you begin cutting off branches that are blocking the sun; you will view things much differently. Know that you can do anything that you put your mind to and that there is nothing in this world that you can't achieve. Taking a one step forward to take two steps back isn't the way to live your life, so begin to let go of things. You weren't put on this Earth to fail, and it's time to be the amazing woman that we know you are meant to be.

Personality Development

Personality development by definition is the development of the organized pattern of behaviors and attitudes that make a person distinctive. Personality development occurs by the ongoing interaction of temperament, character, and environment.

When it comes to a person's personality, some will argue it has nothing to do with your environment while others will say it has everything to do with it. Depending on where you stand on this subject, you could also believe it cannot be changed. Since personality is the typical pattern of an individual, this means it is also unique. There aren't two people with the exact same personality. With that being said, personality can be changed depending on a person's willingness and need to do so. Whenever I hear someone has a good personality, I automatically assume this means they possess a few different qualities, which are considered respectable. It could be that they're likable; maybe they're interesting, or maybe they're just pleasant to be around. Mostly everyone would rather others see their good qualities, despite any bad ones they possess. Through the years I've met people who may have been stunningly beautiful on the outside, but on the inside, they weren't very likable at all. The dislikable parts are the things most people will attempt to conceal. I can't think of anyone who would want people to view them as emotionally or physically unattractive. Your personality determines how any relationship, regardless of the type, will end up.

As women, often we see another woman's qualities and may harbor some jealousy or envy. Instead of looking within ourselves and figuring out ways to enhance our personalities; we find a way to tear her's down. Why is this? It could be a culmination of things. It could be their upbringing, their insecurities, their financial situation, their level of education, their relationship or anything material. Some women have never experienced someone building them up. Some women have even been raised in households where they were only told they were ugly, stupid, and they would never amount to anything. The long-term effects of this type of verbal abuse can be very damaging to a person's self-esteem. They could develop into angry, abusive individuals themselves and begin to act out in much the same manner towards other women. If their financial situation isn't great and they can't afford the latest fashion while others are wearing designer clothing, it would be difficult to compliment another woman. The root of the resentment lies in seeing others with the things they're unable to afford. Maybe they didn't perform well academically and was told this on many occasions. Ultimately, they may begin believing they can't be as intelligent as some of their female counterparts and excel in academia. Jealousy and envy can stunt your growth in any situation.

Instead of working towards a goal to achieve these things, some women often get stuck feeling sorry for themselves. Once you realize you can achieve anything you put your mind to, you will possess the power you need for personality growth and development. Your personality should be powerful! No, it doesn't define who you are, but it shouldn't be affected by the accomplishments of others. It shouldn't mimic anyone else, and it also shouldn't be changed because of society. Your character should also be powerful! These traits are strengthened by your self-acceptance, self-esteem, and confidence. There is room for growth in all of us. Although some rules for personality development apply to everyone, it is important to remember how these rules are applied is largely dependent upon a person's environment. In some cultures, women are raised to be subservient to men. Women have the same potential as men; we are just programmed to think we don't. While keeping these rules in mind and focusing on your goals and achievements, you will be capable of improving your personality. You should also learn what is needed to develop into the woman you want to become. This will require time as well as commitment, but in the end, it will all be worth it. On the outside, there is only so much you can change or enhance. However, on the inside growth is limitless.

There are many ways to accomplish personality development. There isn't a cheat sheet or magic answer. We have created some tips to assist you with your personal growth. Each tip will not apply the same to everyone but is vital to your process.

The idea is to find what you lack to begin your journey.

1. **Reading.** I can't stress enough the importance of reading. There are many books available for almost everything imaginable. Sometimes, we fall behind on the latest trends and information because we don't take the time out of our schedules to do some research. We spend countless hours on social media and blogs, liking photos, commenting and sharing gossip, but very little time is dedicated to our personal growth. It's challenging to improve anything when you aren't even aware there is an issue. By taking the time to read, you may be able to identify what you're doing incorrectly. Looking at what a celebrity may be wearing, what plastic surgery they've had or who they're in a relationship with will not help you with your development. In fact, it could do more harm than good. You may become envious of the things they have instead of focusing on what they did to attain them. You should also expand your interests. Some genres of books are for entertainment

purposes only while others are written to assist you with some aspects of your life. It could be business, finances, love, building your credit or anything along those lines. Sometimes, reading has to be informational and not only to replace some other form of entertainment. You may not think you'll enjoy a self-help book until you read it and it shows you a way to improve an area of your life. Also, instead of surfing social media for gossip, search for things that will assist you in your daily lives. By searching, hashtags on social media is a great way to find posts related to a specific interest. So, grab a pen and pad next time you are tempted to read gossip and write down some useful hashtags.

2. **Meeting People.** The goal shouldn't be only to meet people but to meet someone you can exchange information with and from who you can learn. While meeting other people, you'll be exposed to many different cultures and different ways of handling things in your life. To broaden your horizon, you have to step out of your comfort zone and stop leaning only on what may be familiar to

you. You'll be surprised how much you can learn by being open to learning new things.

3. **Attitude.** You should always try to maintain a positive attitude. If you are always negative, you'll find you won't get very far. People will grow tired of your complaints and most likely opt out of being in your presence. If you continue to tell yourself things that hinder your growth nothing about your personality will every change. You should maintain a positive outlook as well. Bad energy will bring more bad energy ending in disaster. To move forward, you cannot stand still. Sometimes you have to let go of things you love when they are causing you more harm than good. To think positively, you have to challenge yourself. It's not always comfortable, and some people prefer to wallow in sorrow. At some point though, you will have to pick yourself up and move along. Adverse circumstances will always exist; no one lives a perfect life. It doesn't mean you shouldn't acknowledge something causing you to be uncomfortable or upset. It merely means

you should make sense of these things and
then you'll be able to build the strength
needed to combat them.

4. **Acceptance and Perseverance.** Since life
   doesn't always go the way we plan, we have
   to accept 'bad things do happen to good
   people' and consider these issues more of a
   lesson. These bumps in the road have a
   purpose. By viewing them as an opportunity
   to become wiser, you're on your way to
   becoming resilient. You must turn these
   lessons into fuel and use them productively.
   You also need to believe in yourself.
   Whenever you have dreams and goals, show
   your capabilities as well as your talents.
   Once you accept your flaws for what
   they've given you instead of what they've
   taken away; you'll be better equipped for
   your personality growth. Instead of feeling
   sorry for yourself when things don't go the
   way you've planned, do what you can to
   make the best of the situation. Learn how to
   avoid making the same mistakes. You are
   here to evolve, so take notes!

5. **Support and Inspiration.** Life is always a little easier when you are blessed with the backing of others. It is also good to obtain inspiration from someone who can empathize with you or your situation. It never hurts to be encouraged with positivity. To understand their pitfalls can help you go in another direction. To have support from friends and family is great, but they may not always be available. If so, look for others who may be able to provide you with a little boost in the right direction. Just as you need support, others do as well. So, don't forget to be supportive of others because you never know when you may need their help. It's always great to have a cheerleader in your corner.

6. **Being Yourself.** Often, we change into whatever we think people want us to be. Changing who you are for others can become a daunting task and an endless cycle of making the wrong choices. When you strive to fit in or be accepted by others, you will almost always fail. Each person is unique, and you should want to stand out

for your greatness and not become someone else's shadow. On the outside, they may appear to have a perfect life, when on the inside they could be broken. This is why you should focus on you and your needs instead of everyone else's.

7. **Respect.** Some people never learn how to be respectful. They can go their entire lives thinking that inappropriate behavior is correct. Eventually, you will see that you are treated the way you treat others. By being disrespectful, you will most likely receive that in return. At the top of key components on this list, respect of others and respect for yourself will improve your personality the most and is extremely necessary for the proper development.

8. **Confidence.** Self-confidence is imperative. As women, we are often not one hundred percent comfortable with our outside appearance. Often time, these feelings of discomfort are not solely a vanity issue. Regardless of your physical appearance, you have to build your confidence from within.

You can't allow anyone's negative opinion of your look make you feel like you're less of a woman. It may sound silly, but I find that looking in a mirror and telling myself that I'm smart and beautiful helps build my confidence. After a while, no one will ever be able to convince you of anything different. Once you act, look, dress, and speak confidently, everyone will look at you the way that you look at yourself.

9. **Listening and Communicating.** Good communication is the key to successful relationships, whether it be platonic, professional or romantic. We all possess the ability to listen, and this is a trait that everyone should have. Being the loudest doesn't make you the smartest. When you listen patiently and remove your prejudices or feelings, you will begin to listen effectively thus improving your personality. It is just as important to communicate effectively as well. If you are too loud or a little rude, most of what you say during a conversation will go in one ear and out of the other. You have to learn to gauge and

maintain the proper tone in accordance with the setting of which you are speaking. You have to develop a style that will get your thoughts and words across without forcing the other person to become defensive. Doing so is even more important for women because we are often perceived to respond based upon emotions. This often leads to a lack of clarity in our message. By focusing on this clarity, you will soon begin to eliminate any confusion in which your message and meaning can be easily lost.

10. **Leaving the Past in the Past.** We often carry unnecessary baggage from past experiences; whether it's a result of trauma or heartbreak. We have all made mistakes, and because of this, you have to let it go or else you won't be able to grow. To prepare yourself for the great things in your future, you have to learn from the mistakes, including how to forgive, and move on. Your future will look much brighter once you walk from underneath the dark cloud of past issues.

11. **Gossip.** As a society, we are often caught up in the desire to be the first to know something; to get the scoop and this often leads to gossip. On the surface, it seems innocent enough, but in reality, gossip often tends to be the discussion of someone else's downfalls or troubles. The problem with this is no one, including you, likes for their private issues to be the topic of someone else's discussion. There's nothing about it that feels right. It is important that you are always classy and refrain from discussing matters that simply aren't your business. On those occasions you may be pulled into idle gossip, make sure you tactfully decline to comment. Have enough self-respect to remove yourself from situations that keep you wrapped up in other people's drama. The less nonsense you have on the brain, the more free space you have for learning.

12. **Rational Behavior.** By nature, it is often easy to allow emotions to dictate our actions and decision-making; especially in times of heated exchanges. While emotions are important and you should feel free to

express them, you have to remember there are consequences for all of your actions and you will benefit when you take the time to think before reacting.

13. **Minding Your P's and Q's.** There's an adage that says "it's not what you say, it's how you say it"; which holds true in both tone and message. We've all at one time, or another, fallen victim to our mouths getting us in trouble. If you're not in a humorous situation, avoid sarcasm and foul or inappropriate language. This rule applies doubly in professional situations. Represent yourself the way you want to be seen by staying on point and avoiding mishaps.

14. **Dressing Appropriately.** Yes, it's true that you shouldn't judge a book by its cover. You have the right to dress in any manner you see fit, but the truth of the matter is we live in a judgemental world. You will most definitely be judged by what you are wearing, so choose your clothes carefully. Your clothes say a lot about you and regardless of the style of dress you choose,

make sure they express who you are. Your presentation has to be on point. Make sure your clothing is clean, neat and fit properly; doing so will benefit you in the end.

15. **Knowing Yourself.** It's imperative that you know who are you are in life; not just your name, or your physical description, but who you are as an individual. You must be conscious of your thoughts and feelings, and take note of your abilities and flaws. Truly knowing yourself is often overlooked because we fail to take the time to look inside of ourselves. You'd be surprised how much you learn about yourself by taking the time to figure it all out. Study yourself. Learn yourself. Love yourself.

16. **Fear.** Overcoming one's fears is never easy, but it is essential to your well-being. You will only hold yourself back if you are always afraid of moving forward. Knowing your limitations is one thing, but you never want to allow fear to be the reason for your failures. Fear can be your biggest enemy. There are many opportunities we fail to take

full advantage of because we are afraid we will fail. The sense of security you get from backing down from a challenge will foster the bad habits that will stunt your growth. At the onset, it may not feel like it, but failure is always better than not trying at all. You won't get everything right the first time, but don't ever let that be the reason you stop trying.

17. **Fun.** Having a little fun is important. It is commendable to be career or goal driven, but you must always remember that reaching your goals must not come at the expense of your happiness. Laughing is good for the soul, and it can also serve to create deeper connections with the people in your life. Do your best to avoid judgment and approach life from a more optimistic point of view. Always smile as much as possible and relax. In the end, you will learn that maintaining a good mood will assist you in dealing with other issues more appropriately.

18. **Meditation.** Meditation can have

extraordinary power over our lives. Taking time to focus your thoughts will bring about inner peace and a fuller understanding of what you want out of life.

19. **Your Opinion.** It is of the utmost importance to take in the information surrounding you and form your own opinions. Never let someone tell you that you need to think the way they do to be correct. What's important to you, may not be important to the next person, but it is a crucial part of your development and happiness. An opinion not only shapes who you are but having one ultimately makes you much more passionate.

20. **Learning to Love.** For as clichéd and trivial as it may sound, we all need love in our lives; and not just in a romantic way. We need love to connect us to others and motivate us in positive ways. That's not to say that everyone you meet in life will leave a positive impression, but you can't let your bad experiences with certain people prevent you from enjoying those who positively

impact you.

21. **Forgiveness.** No one ever said that forgiving someone who has wronged you is easy. In fact, it's quite difficult, but it's something you have to do for your well-being. The key is to accept that you can never erase the past, and there's nothing you can do to change what has happened to you. However, you can choose not to focus on it any longer and stop allowing it to prevent you from moving forward. Simply put, holding onto the past, keeps you in the past and holding onto anger keeps you in pain.

22. **Being Defensive and Constructive Criticism.** It is no secret it's hard to have your flaws pointed out by others. Unfortunately, your daily interaction with others makes it inevitable to happen. Recognizing the difference between unnecessary criticism and constructive criticism is important. Even though at times it is tough to accept criticism as constructive; it sometimes serves to better us. Learn how to tell the difference between the two and

address them accordingly. So, instead of becoming defensive, you have to learn to take the criticism and turn it into fuel for growth. Never let your emotions limit your ability to grow. You never want to be the person no one can talk to without the fear of you lashing out.

23. **Being A Leader.** Learn to take whatever knowledge you have and apply it in the most efficient way possible. Once you become an authority on a subject, you will possess the knowledge to pass it on to others. It is very rewarding to teach someone something they may not have had the opportunity to learn. Your ultimate goal is to become the type of leader that others will voluntarily follow. Be consistent, be decisive and be respectful; and others will undoubtedly be drawn to you and your message.

24. **Turning Nos Into Yeses.** One thing you never want to do is give up. Regardless of how tough things may get, you have to keep going. Keep trying, and keep working on yourself. No one ever made it to the top

without a couple no's. The difference between them and others is regardless of how many doors were shut in their faces; they didn't give up. They continued to knock on doors until one opened and let them in. Eventually, you will get a yes, but you must stay encouraged and keep trying until your time comes.

25. **Purpose.** Take comfort in knowing that there is a purpose for you and your life. While you may not have discovered what it is as of yet, trust me there is one. One simple way to start you on the path of your purpose is to take stock of the things for which you have a real passion. You will soon notice that the rewards for performing these types of tasks to completion are more significant than others. Discovering your purpose in life most certainly won't be easy, but the journey to finding it will be worth it when you can walk in your truth. Once you have found your purpose, you will notice how much more focused you are in both your personal and professional life. Being focused on your purpose will ultimately

guide you to develop a more engaging personality.

26. **Living Your Life.** We all have been guilty of going through the motions or worrying more and living less. Sometimes we move so quickly through life we forget to take the time to live. If you continue on this path, life will pass you by, and you'll have nothing to show for it other than being overworked and stressed. Once you consciously begin to live your life, you will create and attract exciting opportunities. You should never neglect your responsibilities, but at the same time, you should never neglect 'me-time.' It is essential for your development.

27. **Wasting Time.** It's safe to say that if you examined your life, you would find countless situations where you wasted time dedicating energy to things that didn't elevate you in any way. Personality development is something that will take a lot of time and effort, but you won't be able to improve if you spend too much time on random tasks. The key is to realize what is

and isn't important. The easiest way to decide if an activity is wasting your time is to ask yourself if it is helping you move forward or towards a goal. If the answer is no, then it is an absolute waste of time, regardless if it is an activity, job, friendship or relationship. The more time you spend on unfulfilling undertakings, the less time you have to dedicate yourself to what matters most in your life.

28. **Focus on Success.** It is very easy to focus more on your failures than your successes. You must realize that failure is not final or fatal. Fresh from a failure, it's hard to believe, but success is bred from failure. If you don't take advantage of the power in failure, you will never succeed. The most successful people have been able to turn their failures into successes by determining where they went wrong and avoiding the same pitfalls in future endeavors. None of your failures have ended your life, so you can't allow them to discourage you. Primarily, failure gives us another chance to return much stronger, wiser and smarter. Whatever

you do, don't let failure destroy you.

29. **Education.** The importance of education has been stressed to many of us since grade school. Yet, we don't always appreciate its value outside of our career goals. While career goals are important, education will also provide you with the skills and tools you need to survive in everyday life. To be entirely clear, education is not only found in the halls of traditional schools and college campuses. If you have the means and inclination to attend an institution of higher learning, then you should certainly not hesitate to enroll and take full advantage of all it has to offer. However, should college not be in your plan, you can continue learning by finding a mentor, attending seminars and utilizing online research tools. Regardless of how you choose to receive your education, the key is never to stop learning.

30. **Independence.** There much joy to be found in taking control of your destiny and standing on your own feet. Much like most

good things, there are challenges to be found in independence, but being self-reliant far outweighs any of them. There is comfort in the safety-net of others supporting you, and there is empowerment in taking care of your responsibilities. You need to work hard, look after your finances and set yourself up for the future. Independence means that regardless of what is thrown your way, you will be able to withstand it without crumbling. Curve balls will be thrown at you left and right. Do you have the ability to get out of the way or to catch them and throw them back? If you think back to the lessons learned as a child, they happened to prepare you to stand on your own. There is no better time to do so than now!

In summation, you can only grow if you are willing to put forth the effort. There will always be obstacles placed in front to stop you. The forces behind you will attempt to pull you in the opposite direction of progress. These deterrents come dressed as friends and family, in the form of money and opportunity; and most damning of all self-doubt. You only get one life, and it is much better to live it fully with a well-developed personality. Stop letting envy and jealously handicap you; you are much better than that. Build yourself up, so no one can ever tear you down. Stay positive. Keep your eye on the prize and reach for the moon.

Look in the mirror and say this aloud every morning:

You are smart.
You are beautiful.
You are wise.
You are confident.
You are successful.
You are amazing.
You are a winner.
You are great.
And don't ever let someone convince you of anything different!

"Success is not final; failure is not fatal: it is the courage to continue that counts."

—*Winston S. Churchill*

Hazel-E, birth name Arica Adams, is popularly known for her role on VH1's hit reality series *Love & Hip Hop: Hollywood*. As a breakout cast member, she is widely celebrated for her stance on self-respect and loyalty. A former celebrity publicist, Hazel-E grew up a military girl and graduated from Southwest Texas State University with a Bachelor of Arts degree in Mass Communications-Electronic Media. As a member of Alpha Kappa Alpha Sorority, she created her public relations company Hazel Eyez PR in 2006 followed by her branding and marketing agency Girl Code Incorporated in 2014.

CPSIA information can be obtained
at www.ICGtesting.com
Printed in the USA
FFOW04n1434080517
35440FF